Skill Lessons & Activities

Getting Along with Others

Teaching Social Effectiveness to Children

Nancy F. Jackson
Donald A. Jackson
Cathy Monroe

Research Press / 2612 North Mattis Avenue / Champaign Illinois 61820

9 8 7 6 5 4 3   87 86 85

Permission is granted to reproduce the Home Notes and Homework forms
for any noncommercial use.
All other rights reserved.
Printed in the United States of America.
No other part of this book may be reproduced by mimeograph or any other means
without the written permission of the publisher.
Excerpts may be printed in connection with published reviews in periodicals without express permission.

Research and program development efforts leading to the creation of these materials were supported, in part,
by Grant No. G007804996 from the Office of Special Education, U.S. Department of Education,
through Children's Behavioral Services in Reno, Nevada.
However, these materials do not necessarily represent the policy of the Federal Government,
and no endorsement by it should be assumed.

Copies of this book may be ordered from the publisher at the address given on the title page.

ISBN 0-87822-268-5
ISBN 0-87822-270-7 (2-volume set)

Library of Congress Catalog Card Number 82-62611

Contents

Introduction

Instructions for Using Skill Lessons and Activities

THIS PUBLICATION is designed to accompany the Program Guide from *Getting Along with Others: Teaching Social Effectiveness to Children*. For each of the 17 skills there is a session outline highlighting the skill lesson and indicating optional items including relaxation training, snack time, activity, Home Note, and Homework. In addition to the outline there are separate sheets or scripts for each of the optional items. Your reading of Chapters 3, 4, 5, 6, and 7 of the Guide should have given you a clear idea of how to use these materials.

Use of the Session Outline

As discussed in Chapter 5 of the Guide, the session outline provides scripted dialogue and instructions to lead you through the 2-hour format. You can prepare to teach a session by reading the session outline; it pulls together the suggestions from the Guide in terms of schedule, materials, techniques to use, and behaviors to look for. While it is not intended to be read or memorized and used verbatim, it does provide a clear model for you to imitate. The amount of time devoted to each part of the session outline in our demonstration groups is shown in Chapter 1.

Session 1 differs from the others in that it introduces the program in addition to teaching a specific core skill. The Session 1 Outline includes a script for explaining rules and procedures of the program, as well as some other information basic to the children's participation. Sessions 16 and 17 also differ since they include items related to a party. The script is designed for use of the complete package with a small group. You can make adaptations for a larger group.

Purpose of the Optional Activities

At this point it's worth differentiating again the core components and elements from the optional ones. The core components and elements include: (1) commitment to positive interactions in general; (2) careful definition and clarification of behavioral expectations; (3) introduction of new skills according to the skill lesson in the session outlines; and (4) careful and consistent use of the Teaching Strategies. The optional elements (relaxation training, snack time, activities, Home Notes, Homework, and free play) are designed to enhance the core components.

You must carefully plan opportunities for the children to practice and firmly establish their new skills. Your skill definition and presentation will have provided a strong foundation; still, much more is needed to ensure that the children will draw on their new abilities in stressful situations where, more often than not, existing responses did not solve problems and often even created new ones. The Teaching Strategies provide you with the protocols for strengthening and shaping social interaction skills, but to do so requires that you be in situations with the children where problem behaviors occur. This is the reason for the optional elements of the program: to create *teaching opportunities*. They are described as optional not because they serve a less important function, but because they may be adapted or even deleted as long as you have other ways of ensuring intensive practice and refinement.

To make the most of practice opportunities in the optional activities or naturally occurring situations, you must have specific training targets in mind. Watch for individual children to display improvements or problems with their target behaviors. Plan on emphasizing the day's lesson, e.g., after teaching Skill 6: Interrupting a Conversation, be especially ready to stop interruptions and use a Teaching Strategy to have the children practice waiting for a pause and saying "Excuse me." Don't hesitate to deal with the spurious incidents at hand. For example, if a child spills his juice and begins to cry, go ahead and use the problem-solving sequence with the child, even though it may not be his target behavior or a lesson you have yet taught.

The following list of behaviors is designed to help you prepare for the unexpected. This list is not all-inclusive, but it can help you prepare for the opportunities for incidental teaching that most frequently occur in each optional activity. You should find that children are more capable of applying a new skill to new situations they encounter if you have helped them through several different experiences with the skill. Use this list, then, as a guide to finding teaching opportunities.

Homework Completion and Free Play

Homework Completion

Taking responsibility – Since children have an assignment to do on their own, they have an opportunity *to be honest* about what they've done and to *accept consequences with a good attitude*.

Solving problems – Since some children have a problem remembering to do or bring their homework, this is a good opportunity to use the *problem-solving sequence* to work through strategies for bringing it.

Following directions – Since there are competing preferred activities going on, it is often difficult for children to *follow directions* to work on their Homework, stay seated, or keep their eyes on their papers.

Free Play

Joining in – As children choose partners and games and begin playing, they have opportunities for *joining in* and *starting conversations and keeping them going*.

Cooperating – Children frequently have trouble during this type of activity with being bossy or not *sharing* and *taking turns*. They can work on *ask, not tell; say nice things; let others decide; let others talk; and let others do fun things*.

Solving problems – A variety of mishaps, such as missing game pieces, too many players for a game, or differing ideas about rules can make this a good setting for going through the *problem-solving sequence*.

Keeping a good attitude – Losing games, being sent back in a board game, or other frustrating events can test children's abilities to maintain a *good attitude*.

Following directions – The unstructured nature of this time can encourage horseplay. You may need to give a variety of directions, and watch for target behaviors such as *hands to self* and *use an inside voice*.

Relaxation

Keeping a calm body – Relaxation teaches basics to *keeping a calm body* and *solving problems*.

Following directions – Since children are being given a number of directions, this is a good time to watch for the behavior.

Keeping hands to self – Children are often tempted to touch other children or furniture during this time.

Snack Time

Following group rules – Since snack time is somewhat less structured than the lesson, it often provides opportunities to see and work on many presenting problems, including the group rules that represent basic classroom survival behavior such as *keeping a good attitude, keeping hands to self, using an inside voice*, and *following directions*.

Using conversation skills – Encourage children to talk during snack time so that they can practice *saying*

nice things, joining in, interrupting appropriately*, and *starting a conversation and keeping it going*.

Cooperating – There are often problems during snack time that require children to practice cooperation, e.g., too little juice or snacks, two children wanting the same job, impatience or jealousy about receiving snacks. Thus, *sharing; offering to help; compromising; asking, not telling; taking responsibility just for myself; letting others decide; letting others talk*; and *solving problems* are easily worked with during snack time.

Activity Time

Activity scripts note the skills for which they were designed to provide practice. The less-structured nature of activity time also makes it a good time to watch for behaviors listed here under Free Play and Snack Time.

Home Notes

Following group rules – Since this is conducted as a small-group activity, the group rules apply and should be practiced, including *following directions, keeping a good attitude, raising hand with a quiet mouth, looking at the speaker*, and *keeping hands to self*.

Saying nice things – The children are required to *give* one another *Positive Feedback* for their accomplishments during this time.

Notes about Some of the Optional Activities

The items marked Activity may need your special consideration regarding adaptation. If you find that one of these would not be appropriate for your setting and/or group, you may want to drop it and create something of your own or repeat another activity given. Several of the activities are appropriate for more than one skill. The activity sheets are keyed so that you will know which activities are appropriate for particular skills.

You may wish to substitute an outdoor activity. Outdoor play can provide many opportunities for working on all kinds of social behavior. If you're looking for a substitute but the weather doesn't permit outdoor time, choose fairly unstructured indoor projects on which three to four children can work together to produce the finished product or choose toys or games that require children to work together to build or make things.

All except two of the Relaxation Scripts are intended to be used with more than one skill. Each session outline specifies which Relaxation Script is to be used.

Since the Relaxation Scripts are placed with the session in which they are first used, you will have to pick them up from that place for use with the other skills. For example, Relaxation Script 1 is used with Skills 1 and 2, but the script is placed with materials for Session 1.

You can choose to make the Relaxation Scripts more relevant by substituting one or more paragraphs providing specific examples pertaining to your children. If you do choose to think of new situations for relaxation, please follow this outline:

1. Think of the new situation.
2. Describe how it feels.
3. Tense muscles and relax.
4. Take a deep breath and say the words, "I AM CALM."
5. Think of the situation and stay relaxed.

See Chapter 5 of the Guide for further details about how to use relaxation training.

Session 1

Introduction to the Program & Skill 1: Introducing

YOU MAY SUBSTITUTE naturally occurring events (lunch time, art projects, etc.) for items marked with an asterisk. Be sure to incidentally teach the day's skill, target behaviors, and the behaviors listed whether you use these activities or others. Remember that the dialogue provided in the session outlines (except for the lesson itself) is intended to be a model, not read or memorized verbatim. Read the dialogue over for main points and use your own spontaneous style.

Introduction to Program

Introduce yourself and pass out name tags (if this get-acquainted segment is needed).

Teacher 1:
Welcome. My name is _____ and this is _____. We're going to be meeting together (tell children when, how often, and how many times) and learning some things that can help us make new friends, solve problems, and get along better with other people. Once you have learned these things, you can decide to use them with people at home and at school to make things go more easily for you. To help us get to know one another's names, we are each going to wear name tags today.

(Pass out 3 x 5-inch cards and felt pens and have each child write his/her name on the card.)

Introduce rules.

Teacher 1 or 2:
Before we begin today's lesson, we need to explain some things about how we behave and work in this group. First of all, in order to make our group go smoothly, we need to have a few rules.

(Display Rule Board made according to example in Chapter 3.)

Ask children to read rules.

Teacher 1 or 2:
Who would like to read the first rule?

(Call on child giving eye contact and raising hand quietly; praise appropriate behavior.)

Good.

Define rules and ask children for rationales for rules.

Teacher 1 or 2:
(Go over each rule, defining it in terms of its compo-

nents; demonstrate examples of following each rule, if that seems appropriate.)

(Be certain to define and demonstrate good attitude as follows.)

Now we're going to show you what we mean by a good attitude. I want you to watch my face and see if you think I have a good attitude or not.

(Smile and pleasantly look at children.)

What kind of attitude was that?
(children respond or are prompted)
Right, that was a good attitude. I had a pleasant face, and I looked right at you. Now, see what kind of attitude this is.

(Frown, grimace, roll eyes, and look away.)

Was that a good attitude?
(children respond or are prompted)
Right. I had a grouchy face and needed to get a pleasant face and start looking at you. Now listen to my voice and see what kind of attitude I have.

(Use a pleasant voice.)

All right, I will.
(children respond or are prompted)
Right. I had a pleasant voice, so you could tell I had a good attitude. Let's try it again. What kind of attitude is this?

(Whine and sigh.)

All right, I will.
(children respond or are prompted)
Right. I didn't have a pleasant voice, so that wasn't a good attitude. To have a good attitude, you need to look at the person and have a pleasant face and voice. Why do you think it is a good idea to have these rules?
(children respond or are prompted)
Following these rules is very important. When we follow the rules, everything goes smoothly, we have more fun, and we get to move on to other things faster, such

as snacks or recess. You will be earning snacks by following the rules.

Introduce Positive Feedback.

Teacher 1 or 2:
When you are following the rules and learning new behaviors, we will let you know exactly what you are doing right. This is called Positive Feedback. For instance, right now _____, _____, and _____ are looking right at me, so I can tell they're listening. I just gave them Positive Feedback. Sometimes, we will ask you to give Positive Feedback and tell other children exactly what they did right in part of our lesson.

Introduce and role play Sit and Watch.

Teacher 1:
Sometimes people have trouble following the rules. When this happens, we use a procedure called Sit and Watch. We will show you how it works. Let's pretend that (Teacher 2) is having trouble following the rules.

(Teacher 2 pokes neighboring child. Use Sit and Watch with your teaching partner; see Chapter 4 to review procedure.)

Explain snack time.

Teacher 1 or 2:
During each session we have snack time. The way each of you earns snack is by following our group rules, paying attention, practicing, and volunteering during the group. If you don't follow the rules or practice during the group, _____ or I will ask you to practice during snack time, and then you'll miss part of snack.

To make sure you earn snack, what do you need to do? (children respond or are prompted)
And when do we have snack?
(children respond or are prompted)

(Be sure to praise children for appropriate answers.)

*Relaxation Training

In addition to today's skill and children's individual target behaviors, give special attention to keeping a calm body, solving problems, following directions, and keeping hands to self.

Introduce relaxation training.

Teacher 1 or 2:
Now we are going to do something that we will do each time we meet in the group. It is called relaxation. Relaxation teaches us how to be calm and make our bodies feel relaxed. I would like each of you to find a spot on the floor and lie down, making sure that you are not touching anyone or anything. Lie with your arms at your side, close your eyes, and follow all the instructions.

(Have someone turn off lights.)

Lead relaxation training.

(Use Relaxation Script 1.)

Introduce skill lesson.

Teacher 1 or 2:
Each time we meet we will learn a new skill. We will tell you about it, show you what it looks like, and have you practice it.

Skill Lesson 1

● Introduce skill and list components.

Teacher 1:
Today we are going to talk about introducing yourself to someone you don't know and introducing two people who don't know each other. To introduce yourself, you:
- Use a pleasant face and voice.
- Look at the person.
- Tell the person your name.
- Ask for the person's name.

To introduce two people who don't know each other, you:
- Use a pleasant face and voice.
- Look at each person.
- Tell each person the other's name.

. . . .

● Role play appropriate example.

Teacher 1:
This is the right way to introduce yourself. I'm going to introduce myself to a new student.
Hi, my name is _____. What's yours?

Teacher 2:
I'm _____. Nice to meet you.

● Ask children for behavior components of skill.

Teacher 1:
How did you know that was the right way to introduce yourself?
(children respond or are prompted)

● Role play inappropriate example.

Teacher 1:
This is the wrong way to introduce yourself. I'm going to introduce myself to a new student.
Hey, are you new here?

Teacher 2:
Yeah.

● Ask children for behavior components of skill.

Teacher 1:
What should have happened to make that the right way to introduce yourself?
(children respond or are prompted)

. . . .

● Role play appropriate example.

Teacher 1:
This is the right way to introduce two people who don't

know each other. I am with (Teacher 2), who is a new student, and my friend walks up.
Hi, _____. _____, this is (Teacher 2).
(Teacher 2), this is _____.

● Ask children for behavior components of skill.

Teacher 1:
How did you know what was the right way to introduce two people who don't know each other?
(children respond or are prompted)

● Role play inappropriate example.

Teacher 1:
This is the wrong way to introduce two people who don't know each other. I am with (Teacher 2), who is a new student, and my friend walks up.
Hi, _____, do you want to play?

● Ask children for behavior components of skill.

Teacher 1:
What should have happened to make that the right way to introduce two people who don't know each other?
(children respond or are prompted)

. . . .

● Ask children to role play.

Teacher 1:
Now it is your turn to role play. (Assign role play situation.) I am going to call on someone who has been working really hard in the group by (specific on-task behaviors). _____ has been working really hard the whole time by (appropriate behaviors) and looks ready to be the first one to role play. _____, this is your role play.

(Describe the role play you have previously selected for this child from the role play sheet behind this session outline. Have each child role play the skill *correctly* at least one time.)

● Ask children to give Positive Feedback.

Teacher 1 or 2:
Good role playing. Who can give _____ *some Positive Feedback on his/her role play?*

(Call on child who is volunteering and paying attention.)

. . . .

● Ask children for rationales for using skill.

Teacher 1:
Why do you think it is important to introduce yourself and

others?
(children respond or are prompted)

Children:
- You will know the person's name.
- You will seem friendlier.
- People will like you because you are polite.
- You will have more friends.

. . . .

● **Lead children through reality check.**

Teacher 1:
Sometimes you might try really hard to introduce yourself or others, *and this might happen.* I'm going to introduce myself to a new student.
Hi, my name is _____. What's yours?

Teacher 2:
Oh, leave me alone. Get lost.

Teacher 1:
You just did everything right to introduce yourself. *What should you do if this happens to you?*
(children respond or are prompted)

Children:
- Take a deep breath to get calm.
- Keep a good attitude.
- Ignore.
- Try again later.
- Wait till a better time.
- Go find a friendlier person.

---

*Snack Time

In addition to today's skill and children's individual target behaviors, give special attention to following group rules, using conversation skills, cooperating, and solving problems.

Decide which children have earned all of snack.

Children may earn the entire snack or only a smaller portion if they join the snack in progress. Keep in mind how much difficulty a child has had following rules or practicing during the lesson and relaxation time to get an idea of how much time the child might need to practice to compensate for missed opportunities.

Dismiss children who have already earned snack time to the snack table.

Teacher 1:
OK, it's snack time now. (Teacher 2), who do you think has really been earning snack today?

Teacher 2:
Well, _____ has been really following the rules, having a still body, volunteering, and working on (his/her target behavior).

Teacher 1:
Yes, he/she really has. And I think _____ has also done a really good job of (specific behaviors). I'd like (child already named) to go to the snack table and pass out the napkins and (other child named) to go and pass out the cups.

(Continue dismissing children to the snack table by giving Positive Feedback for their accomplishments and assigning them a task at the snack table. If some chil-

dren have not earned all of snack, have them practice as follows.)

Teacher 1:
_____, you need to sit here with me and practice (volunteering, keeping hands to self, etc.).

(Ask children questions from the lesson, have them role play, or do relaxation to give them opportunities to practice behaviors that were problematic during relaxation and/or the lesson. As the children practice, watch for a good attitude and effort in practicing and determine when each child seems to have made up for lost opportunities and achieved an acceptable level of competence in the skill or rule following.)

Ask children to clean up snack area.

Teacher 1:
OK, snack time is over now. We need to clean up.
_____, would you get the garbage can and bring it around so everyone can throw away the garbage.

(Use Positive Feedback and other Teaching Strategies for cooperating and following directions during the cleanup.)

---

*Activity Time

In addition to today's skill and children's individual target behaviors, give special attention to following group rules, using conversation skills, cooperating, and solving problems.

Explain activity for today's lesson.

Teacher 1:
It's time for an activity now. Today we're going to

(describe activity briefly). This is a time for us to practice Introducing.

(Use Activity.)

Ask all the children to help clean up.

Teacher 1:
Now it's time for everyone to help clean up.

(Use Positive Feedback and other Teaching Strategies to help children work well together on cleanup. After cleanup, prompt children to return to circle.)

---

*Home Notes

In addition to today's skill and children's individual target behaviors, give special attention to following group rules and saying nice things.

Explain Home Notes.

Teacher 1:
This is a Home Note.

(Hold up copy of today's Home Note.)

The last 15 minutes of the group is for Home Notes. We will talk about how you did, give you Positive Feedback, and mark your Home Note according to how well you did that day in social skills group. Your parents will mark the bottom section of your Home Note, letting us know how you did at home. Bring that section back with your Homework next time.

Divide children into two groups and explain target behaviors.

Teacher 1:
Each person in the group has special behaviors to work on each time. We have decided on these behaviors because we think they are the things that will help you the most.

(Explain each child's target behaviors, defining them in terms of the components [refer to the Target Behavior Worksheet, Chapter 3]. If more than one child has a certain target behavior, e.g., following directions, define it only once. While waiting to hear his/her own target behaviors, each child must wait patiently and quietly, listening carefully. Try to incorporate examples of children using the behaviors during the group today, giving Positive Feedback whenever possible. Score the target behaviors with "n/a" for today and tell the children about the grading scale you will use next session.)

---

*New Homework

In addition to today's skill and children's individual target behaviors, give special attention to following group rules and saying nice things.

Explain Homework.

Teacher 1 or 2:
At the end of every social skills group you will be given Homework.

(Hold up copy of Homework.)

The Homework questions deal with our lesson for that day. You will need to practice our lesson at home or at school. Use it with someone and then write down what happened. (Younger children may ask their parents to help them write their answers.) It is your responsibility to bring your Homework back completed at the beginning of our next group meeting. If it is completed and returned, you'll get to choose a sticker to put on the Homework Board and have some time to play.

(Display Homework Board made according to example in Chapter 5. If Homework is turned in late, you may want to let child color in one half square.)

Those who complete most of their Homework by the end of all our meetings will get to choose a special prize. At the beginning of each session we will review the Homework you bring back.

Pass out Homework.

Teacher 1:
Here is your Homework. Be sure to do it and bring it back next time. Let's see what it says.

(Read aloud.)

If you need help, ask your parents or some other adult in your home.

Relaxation Script 1

(This script may be used in conjunction with Skills 1 and 2. Please review the section on relaxation training in Chapter 5 of the Guide.)

Before we begin today's lesson, we're going to spend a few minutes learning how to relax our bodies. We are all doing something new here together. Sometimes when we do something new we get nervous or upset and our bodies get tense. Our stomachs might feel upset, our hands might sweat, we might breathe faster, or our muscles might feel tight. Right now we are going to learn how it feels to be tense, and how it feels to be relaxed.

Make a fist with your hands. (pause) Feel how tight the muscles in your arms and hands are. This is called being tense. Now relax your hands.

Now make a fist with your hands and squeeze them as hard as you can while I count to three. (count aloud slowly) One . . . two . . . three. Now relax your hands and feel the tightness leave your arms. It feels good, doesn't it? Now your arms and hands feel soft and loose.

Now I'm going to teach you how to make your whole body feel relaxed just like your arms feel now. Remember how it felt when you tensed your arms? Now you're going to make your whole body tense. Push your head, your shoulders, your arms, your hands, your back, your bottom, your legs, and your feet into the floor as hard as you can. Hold it while I count to three. (count aloud slowly) One . . . two . . . three. Now relax. Your whole body should feel soft, loose, and relaxed. Think about how good it feels when your body is relaxed. (pause)

Now we're going to make our bodies tense again. Push your head, your shoulders, your arms, your hands, your back, your bottom, your legs, and your feet into the floor. Try to put a dent in the floor. Hold it while I count to three. (count aloud slowly) One . . . two . . . three. Now relax and feel your body become soft and calm. (pause)

Taking deep breaths is another way to help our bodies to relax. Place your hand on your tummy. (pause long enough so that all can follow your directions; praise and assist as needed) Now, very slowly, as I count, breathe into your hand. Your tummy should fill up like a balloon and gently push your hand up. (count aloud slowly) One . . . two . . . three. Now as you slowly breathe out, say "I AM CALM." (pause) Relax. Now you feel relaxed. Your body feels soft, loose, and calm. (pause)

Now let's take another deep breath. Place your hand on your tummy. Now, as I count to three, breathe in slowly, then hold it for a second, and say "I AM CALM" as you breathe out. (count aloud slowly) One . . . two . . . three. Hold it. (pause) Now breathe out slowly and say "I AM CALM." See how much better it feels to be calm and relaxed? (pause)

Now I want you to think back about how you felt when you came here today. This was something new for you, and your body might have felt a little tense and upset. Imagine yourself in this new situation. Tighten your muscles and make your whole body tense. Hold it. (count aloud slowly) One . . . two . . . three. (pause) Relax. Now your muscles feel relaxed and your stomach feels calm. (pause) One more time, think about how you felt coming here today, but this time keep your body still and loose. (pause) Place your hand on your tummy. As I count to three, breathe into your hand very slowly. (count aloud slowly) One . . . two . . . three. As you breathe out, say the words "I AM CALM." (pause) Relax. See how much better it feels to be calm and relaxed in a new situation? (pause)

Now I want you to think of another time when you were in a new situation; you might have been speaking in front of your class, visiting the doctor or dentist, or talking to a new student at school. (Pause and give children a chance to think of their own situations.) Imagine yourself in this situation. Your stomach feels upset, your hands and legs are shaking, and your body feels tense. Tighten your muscles and make your whole body tense. Hold it. (count aloud slowly) One . . . two . . . three. Now let go; your body feels soft and relaxed. (pause) Place your hand on your tummy. As I count to three, very slowly breathe into your hand. And as you breathe out, say the words "I AM CALM." (count aloud slowly) One . . . two . . . three. (pause) Relax. One more time, think about being in your new situation, but this time keep your body still and loose. (pause) Place your hand on your tummy. As I count to three, slowly breathe into your hand, and as you breathe out, say the words "I AM CALM." (count aloud slowly) One . . . two . . . three. (pause) Relax. Now your body feels calm and relaxed.

The next time that you begin to feel upset or nervous, remember how you feel right now. You can make your body feel calm and relaxed all the time. When you want to relax, think about your body, take a deep breath, and let go of all the tension. Being calm and relaxed helps you to be comfortable in new situations.

Skill 1: Introducing
Role Plays

Situations Target Behaviors	School Problems (Teacher/Peers)	Neighborhood Problems	Sibling Problems	Parent Problems
Listen Carefully	You're at a new school. You have met three new kids. Now your teacher wants you to introduce them to your mom and dad.	You have just introduced yourself to a new kid. A friend of yours walks by. You need to introduce them to each other.	Your older brother introduces you to some new friends of his. Now your little brother wants to meet them.	Your mom introduces you to the new babysitter. Now she wants you to introduce him to your little sister.
Treat Others Nicely	You're walking home from school with a friend, and a little first-grader joins you. She doesn't know your friend.	You're playing with your best friend. A little neighbor kid comes over and wants to play. They don't know each other.	You have to babysit your little sister and her friend. You don't know her friend's name.	Your dad takes you to the park but says he'd rather read his book than play. While playing alone with your yo-yo, a little girl comes by and stops to watch you.
Join in with Others	Two kids that you don't know are playing a game that you would really like to join.	A friend invites you to a birthday party. He's the only person you know there. You'd like to meet the girl near you.	Your brother invites you to get ice cream with him and his two friends. You don't know his friends.	You go with your dad to visit his friends. You don't know the kids, but your dad tells you to go out and play with them.
Keep a Good Attitude	Your classroom has a substitute teacher today. He tells you to introduce him to the three kids sitting near your desk.	Your dad drops you off at the movie where you are to meet a friend. He doesn't show up. You're near a kid your age in line.	Your sister gets sick at her party and goes to bed. You have to entertain her guests. You don't know two of them.	Your mom tells you to help a sick neighbor with her yard work. You don't even know the lady.
Take Responsibility for Self	You are your team's captain. Two of your teammates don't know each other.	Two of your friends at the party you are giving don't know each other.	You've asked your older sister to take you to a friend's house. His mom is out in the yard and hasn't met your sister.	Your dad comes to open house at your school. He wants to ask your teacher some questions but has never met her.
Stay Calm and Relaxed	You met a new kid last week. Today you see him and realize that you have forgotten his name.	Your mom takes you and a friend to the pool. A different friend swims up. Your two friends don't know each other.	Your brother invites you to play with him and two of his friends. You don't know them, and he doesn't introduce you.	You're at the park with your mom. You see your principal there with her kids. Your mom wants to meet her.
Solve Problems	Your classroom has a visitor today. The teacher thinks you know him and asks to be introduced. You don't know him.	Your mom tells you to invite some friends over. You invite two new neighbor kids that your mom doesn't know.	Your sister introduced you to a new friend. You want to ask her to play, but you forgot her name.	You start to introduce your dad to two new friends. You have forgotten one of their names.

Skill 1: Introducing
Activity

The materials needed are:

1. A set of cards naming movie or cartoon characters or animals that are familiar to the children (there should be as many cards as there are children playing the game).
2. A pencil and piece of paper for each child.
3. Small prizes (stickers, prizes from caramel corn boxes).

To begin, have each child pick one card, without showing it to anyone or telling anyone the name on the card. Tell the children to pretend to be the characters named on their cards. The object of the activity is to find out the names of as many of the other children as possible in a set time (10-15 minutes). Children should approach other children and introduce themselves to as many other "characters" as possible.

The rules are:

1. If a child introduces himself/herself correctly by saying, "Hi," telling his/her name, and asking the other person's name, the other person must give his/her name. (The children can write down names on their sheets of paper to help them remember.)
2. If a child fails to introduce himself/herself correctly, the other person doesn't have to give his/her name, and the first child must find someone else to whom he/she can introduce himself/herself.
3. When the allotted time is over, everyone will return to the circle, and each person in turn will read from his/her paper the names of all the characters he/she has met. He/she will then choose two to introduce to each other.
4. Everyone who has learned the character names of at least 3/4 of the other children in the group as evidenced by total number of names on his/her paper will earn a prize.

When children are observed introducing themselves incorrectly or not introducing themselves, use the Teaching Interaction or Ignore-Attend-Praise to help them to practice introducing correctly. Give Positive Feedback for instances of correct introducing.

Skill 1: Introducing
Home Note

Name _____ Instructors _____

During today's lesson we practiced introducing ourselves to someone we don't know and introducing two people who don't know each other.

Today's Objectives	**Target Behaviors**

Today's Objectives

To introduce himself/herself, did the child:

	YES	NO
1. Use a pleasant face and voice?	____	____
2. Look at the person?	____	____
3. Tell the person his/her name?	____	____
4. Ask for the person's name?	____	____

To introduce two people who don't know each other, did the child:

	YES	NO
5. Use a pleasant face and voice?	____	____
6. Look at each person?	____	____
7. Tell each person the other's name?	____	____

Target Behaviors

Score

A. _____ ____

B. _____ ____

C. _____ ____

D. _____ ____

E. _____ ____

Score, using this scale:
1 = Completely satisfied
2 = Satisfied
3 = Slightly satisfied
4 = Neither satisfied nor dissatisfied
5 = Slightly dissatisfied
6 = Dissatisfied
7 = Completely dissatisfied

The best thing your child did today in social skills was _____
_____

- -

Parents – Please Complete This Section and Return
Skill 1: Introducing

Name _____

The following objectives and target behaviors refer to those named above. Please mark or score your child in these areas and have him/her return this bottom section with your signature to the next social skills group.

Did your child meet the objectives of today's lesson at least once this week?

	YES	NO
Objective 1	____	____
Objective 2	____	____
Objective 3	____	____
Objective 4	____	____
Objective 5	____	____
Objective 6	____	____
Objective 7	____	____

Score your child on his/her target behaviors, using the 1-7 scale above:

Target Behavior A _____

Target Behavior B _____

Target Behavior C _____

Target Behavior D _____

Target Behavior E _____

Parent Signature _____ Date _____

Skill 1: Introducing
Homework

Name _____

1. What are at least three things you can do or say to introduce yourself to someone you don't know?

   a. _____
   _____

   b. _____
   _____

   c. _____
   _____

2. Before our next group, introduce yourself to at least one *new* person.

   a. Where were you? _____
   _____

   b. Who did you meet? _____
   _____

   c. What did you say? _____
   _____

   d. What did the other person do or say?_____
   _____

3. Before our next group, introduce two people you know who don't know each other. (Hint: If your teacher and mom/dad haven't met, you could introduce them to each other.)

   a. What did you do and say?_____
   _____

   b. What did they do and say? _____
   _____

Session 2

Skill 2: Following Directions

YOU MAY SUBSTITUTE naturally occurring events (lunch time, art projects, etc.) for items marked with an asterisk. Be sure to incidentally teach the day's skill, target behaviors, and the behaviors listed whether you use these activities or others. Remember that the dialogue provided in the session outlines (except for the lesson itself) is intended to be a model, not read or memorized verbatim. Read the dialogue over for main points and use your own spontaneous style. **Most of the dialogue and instructions are identical from skill to skill. For efficiency you may wish to attend only to the Relaxation Script number and the new information in the Skill Lesson.**

---

*Homework Completion and Free Play

In addition to today's skill and children's individual target behaviors, give special attention to taking responsibility, solving problems, and following directions (during Homework completion), and joining in, cooperating, problem solving, keeping a good attitude, and following directions (during free play).

Collect Homework and the bottom half of Home Notes; oversee free play and Homework completion or practice time.

Teacher 1:
(Scan papers to see which children have satisfactorily completed Homework; put aside Home Notes to check later.)

(children who completed it), you may go now and choose a game to play. (children who have not completed it), it's time for you to finish the Homework (or practice the skill) so that you can join the others.

(For children who habitually do not bring completed Homework, add more written questions or role play practice so that they finish about the same time as free play ends.)

Review Homework with children.

Teacher 1:
(Have children form a circle on the floor.)

Now let's look at the Homework you have done. I'm glad that (children who brought completed work) did their work at home. (a child who brought it), will you read your answer to Question _____?

(Have several children who brought their work read answers; ask for feedback from others. If you are using the Homework Progress Chart, allow children to color in the whole square or place a sticker in the square or color in part of it, depending on whether they brought completed Homework or finished it during free play.)

---

*Relaxation Training

In addition to today's skill and children's individual target behaviors, give special attention to keeping a calm body, solving problems, following directions, and keeping hands to self.

Lead relaxation training.

Teacher 1:
We are going to practice relaxing again. Relaxing will help you learn the new skill and help you face any problem.

(Have children find a place on the floor to lie down. Choose one child to turn off the lights.)

(Use Relaxation Script 1.)

15

Skill Lesson 2

● **Introduce skill and list components.**

Teacher 1:
Today we are going to talk about following directions. To follow directions, you:
▪ Use a pleasant face and voice.
▪ Look at the person giving the directions.
▪ Say "OK."
▪ Start to do what was asked right away.
▪ Do it satisfactorily.
. . . .

● **Role play appropriate example.**

Teacher 1:
This is the right way to follow directions. I'm at school, and my teacher is about to give me some directions.

Teacher 2:
_____, you need to throw your gum away.

Teacher 1:
OK. (gets up right away and throws gum away)

● **Ask children for behavior components of skill.**

Teacher 1:
How did you know that was the right way to follow directions?
(children respond or are prompted)

● **Role play inappropriate example.**

Teacher 1:
This is the wrong way to follow directions. I'm at school, and my teacher is about to give me some directions.

Teacher 2:
_____, you need to throw your gum away.

Teacher 1:
OK. (no eye contact, does not throw gum away; continues what he/she is doing)

● **Ask children for behavior components of skill.**

Teacher 1:
What should have happened to make that the right way to follow directions?
(children respond or are prompted)
. . . .

● **Ask children to role play.**

Teacher 1:
Now it is your turn to role play. (Assign role play situation.) I am going to call on someone who has been working really hard in the group by (specific on-task behaviors).

_____ has been working really hard the whole time by (appropriate behaviors) and looks ready to be the first one to role play. _____, this is your role play.

(Describe the role play you have previously selected for this child from the role play sheet behind this session outline. Have each child role play the skill *correctly* at least one time.)

● **Ask children to give Positive Feedback.**

Teacher 1 or 2:
Good role playing. Who can give _____ *some Positive Feedback on his/her role play?*

(Call on child who is volunteering and paying attention.)
. . . .

● **Ask children for rationales for using skill.**

Teacher 1:
Why do you think it is important to follow directions?
(children respond or are prompted)

Children:
▪ Makes you feel good.
▪ Helps you earn privileges.
▪ Keeps you out of trouble.
▪ Teachers and parents know you are listening.
. . . .

● **Lead children through reality check.**

Teacher 1:
Sometimes you might try really hard to follow directions, *and this might happen.* I'm at school, and my teacher is about to give me some directions.

Teacher 2:
_____, you need to throw your gum away.

Teacher 1:
OK. (gets up right away and throws gum away)

Teacher 2:
It's about time you followed my directions!

Teacher 1:
You just did everything right to follow directions. *What should you do if this happens to you?*
(children respond or are prompted)

Children:
▪ Take a deep breath to get calm.
▪ Keep a good attitude.
▪ Feel good about what you did.
▪ Keep trying.
▪ Make sure you follow directions right away every time.

*Snack Time

In addition to today's skill and children's individual target behaviors, give special attention to following group rules, using conversation skills, cooperating, and solving problems.

Decide which children have earned all of snack.

Children may earn the entire snack or only a smaller portion if they join the snack in progress. Keep in mind how much difficulty a child has had following rules or practicing during the lesson and relaxation time to get an idea of how much time the child might need to practice to compensate for missed opportunities.

Dismiss children who have already earned snack time to the snack table.

Teacher 1:
OK, it's snack time now. (Teacher 2), who do you think has really been earning snack today?

Teacher 2:
Well, _____ has been really following the rules, having a still body, volunteering, and working on (his/her target behavior).

Teacher 1:
Yes, he/she really has. And I think _____ has also done a really good job of (specific behaviors). I'd like (child already named) to go to the snack table and pass out the napkins and (other child named) to go and pass out the cups.

(Continue dismissing children to the snack table by giving Positive Feedback for their accomplishments and assigning them a task at the snack table. If some children have not earned all of snack, have them practice as follows.)

Teacher 1:
_____, you need to sit here with me and practice (volunteering, keeping hands to self, etc.).

(Ask children questions from the lesson, have them role play, or do relaxation to give them opportunities to practice behaviors that were problematic during relaxation and/or the lesson. As the children practice, watch for a good attitude and effort in practicing and determine when each child seems to have made up for lost opportunities and achieved an acceptable level of competence in the skill or rule following.)

Ask children to clean up snack area.

Teacher 1:
OK, snack time is over now. We need to clean up. _____, would you get the garbage can and bring it around so everyone can throw away the garbage.

(Use Positive Feedback and other Teaching Strategies for cooperating and following directions during the cleanup.)

---

*Activity Time

In addition to today's skill and children's individual target behaviors, give special attention to following group rules, using conversation skills, cooperating, and solving problems.

Explain activity for today's lesson.

Teacher 1:
It's time for an activity now. Today we're going to (describe activity briefly). This is a time for us to practice our target behaviors and Following Directions.

(Use Activity.)

Ask all the children to help clean up.

Teacher 1:
Now it's time for everyone to help clean up.

(Use Positive Feedback and other Teaching Strategies to help children work well together on cleanup. After cleanup, prompt children to return to circle.)

---

*Home Notes

In addition to today's skill and children's individual target behaviors, give special attention to following group rules and saying nice things.

Divide children into two groups and work on scoring Home Notes.

Teacher 1:
(a child), we are going to talk about how you did during today's session. Who can give (that child) some Positive Feedback and tell him/her good things about how he/she did on (target behavior)?

(Score the top half of the Home Note while the children are giving Positive Feedback. Ask for specific feedback for each of the child's target behaviors and add to it with comments you want to make, pointing out progress and areas needing improvement.)

(same child), now what do you think was the best thing you did in group today?
(child responds or is prompted)

Teacher 1:
That's good.

(Add specific descriptions of strong points.)

You might also try to (suggestions for improvement). Here is your Home Note.

(Repeat sequence with each child.)

---

*New Homework

In addition to today's skill and children's individual target behaviors, give special attention to following group rules and saying nice things.

Pass out Homework.

Teacher 1:
Here is your Homework. Be sure to do it and bring it back next time. Let's see what it says.

(Read aloud.)

If you need help, ask your parents or some other adult in your home.

Skill 2: Following Directions
Role Plays

Situations / Target Behaviors	School Problems (Teacher/Peers)	Neighborhood Problems	Sibling Problems	Parent Problems
Listen Carefully	Your teacher tells you to clean out your desk, take your test papers home, and do your homework.	You are working for a neighbor to earn money. He tells you to rake the lawn, pull the weeds, and water the flowers.	Your older brother tells you to help clean the back-yard by raking leaves and watering the flowers so you can all go swimming sooner.	Your dad tells you to help your mom dust, mop, and clean the garage.
Treat Others Nicely	The captain of a team you are on at school tells you to wait your turn and not butt up in line.	A neighbor child tattles on you. His mom tells you to keep your hands to your-self and then leaves you alone with him.	It's your older sister's turn to supervise chores. She gives you all of the hard jobs.	Your mom grabs you up off the sofa and yells at you to do your homework.
Join in with Others	Your teacher tells you to choose a partner and lead a game in front of the class.	A neighbor girl's dad comes to your house and asks you to help his daughter with her home-work assignment.	Your older brother tells you to be his partner in a game he's playing with some new friends.	Your dad tells you to intro-duce your new teacher to him and invite her over for dinner.
Keep a Good Attitude	You are reading a story-book because you finished math. Your teacher tells you to help another student with his math.	You are playing in the sprinklers on a friend's lawn. His dad tells you to go home.	Your older sister is baby-sitting you. She tells you to clean up the living room.	You are watching your favorite television show after dinner. Your dad tells you to wash the dishes.
Take Responsibility for Self	Your teacher gives you directions for tomorrow's homework. You have free time right now.	A friend hands you a toy to look at and tells you to give it back as soon as you've looked at it.	Your older brother tells you to finish your home-work before you turn on the television.	Your dad tells you to feed your pets and do your homework before you play with your friends. They are waiting for you.
Stay Calm and Relaxed	Your teacher yells at the whole class to clean up an art activity. She's really angry. But you didn't make the mess.	Your next-door neighbor saw you and a friend throw mud on his fence. He yells at you to clean it up.	Your older sister is giving you directions for doing a really hard math problem.	Your mom is telling how to do a chore you already know how to do. She tells you about three times.
Solve Problems	Your teacher tells you to run an errand for her. You really feel tired today.	A neighbor tells you to get your dog out of her yard. You're really busy playing.	Your brother tells you to clean up the mess you made in his bedroom. You feel really sleepy right now.	Your mom and dad both give you some chores to do at the same time.

Skill 2: Following Directions
Activity

(The activity provided for Skill 9: Sharing can also be used here with Skill 2.)

The materials needed are:

1. Paper, crayons, paints, and/or other items for a drawing or other art project, or
2. Building materials such as Legos, Lincoln Logs, models, or
3. Board games.

Following Directions is appropriately practiced by many activities, including:

1. Playing "Simon Says."
2. Drawing from dictation, i.e., you give a step-by-step description of what the child should do.
3. Completing any complex art project which requires following instructions.
4. Building from directions, e.g., with Legos, Lincoln Logs, models, etc.
5. Playing board games.

Watch for Following Directions during any of the above activities. Following Directions with a good attitude may be tested by asking the child to leave the game to get something or do an undesirable task. Give Positive Feedback to children who follow your instructions right away. Use the appropriate Teaching Strategies to build Following Directions with those children who complain, whine, or make excuses.

Skill 2: Following Directions
Home Note

Name _____ Instructors _____

During today's lesson we practiced following a clearly given direction immediately after it was given and doing it with a good attitude.

Today's Objectives	Target Behaviors

Today's Objectives

To follow directions, did the child:

	YES	NO
1. Use a pleasant face and voice?	_____	_____
2. Look at the person giving the directions?	_____	_____
3. Say "OK"?	_____	_____
4. Start to do what was asked right away?	_____	_____
5. Do it satisfactorily?	_____	_____

Target Behaviors

Score

A. _____ _____
B. _____ _____
C. _____ _____
D. _____ _____
E. _____ _____

Score, using this scale:
1 = Completely satisfied
2 = Satisfied
3 = Slightly satisfied
4 = Neither satisfied nor dissatisfied
5 = Slightly dissatisfied
6 = Dissatisfied
7 = Completely dissatisfied

The best thing your child did today in social skills was _____
_____

- -

Parents – Please Complete This Section and Return
Skill 2: Following Directions

Name _____

The following objectives and target behaviors refer to those named above. Please mark or score your child in these areas and have him/her return this bottom section with your signature to the next social skills group.

Did your child meet the objectives of today's lesson at least once this week?

	YES	NO
Objective 1	_____	_____
Objective 2	_____	_____
Objective 3	_____	_____
Objective 4	_____	_____
Objective 5	_____	_____

Score your child on his/her target behaviors, using the 1-7 scale above:

Target Behavior A _____
Target Behavior B _____
Target Behavior C _____
Target Behavior D _____
Target Behavior E _____

Parent Signature _____ Date _____

Skill 2: Following Directions
Homework

Name _____

1. What are at least four things you can do to show that you are following directions the right way?

   a. _____
   _____

   b. _____
   _____

   c. _____
   _____

   d. _____
   _____

2. Write down a direction your mom or dad gave to you. (What exactly did she or he say?) Then write down what you said and did.

   a. What did the other person say? _____
   _____

   b. What did you say and do? _____
   _____

3. Write down a direction your teacher, babysitter, or some other adult gave to you. (What exactly did he or she say?) Then write down what you said and did.

   a. What did the other person say? _____
   _____

   b. What did you say and do? _____
   _____

4. What do you think you should do and/or say if someone gives you a direction, but you don't want to do it? (Tell why you answered this way.)

   a. What do you think you should do and/or say? _____
   _____

   b. Why? _____
   _____

Session 3

Skill 3: Giving and Receiving Positive Feedback

YOU MAY SUBSTITUTE naturally occurring events (lunch time, art projects, etc.) for items marked with an asterisk. Be sure to incidentally teach the day's skill, target behaviors, and the behaviors listed whether you use these activities or others. Remember that the dialogue provided in the session outlines (except for the lesson itself) is intended to be a model, not read or memorized verbatim. Read the dialogue over for main points and use your own spontaneous style. **Most of the dialogue and instructions are identical from skill to skill. For efficiency you may wish to attend only to the Relaxation Script number and the new information in the Skill Lesson.**

---

*Homework Completion and Free Play

In addition to today's skill and children's individual target behaviors, give special attention to taking responsibility, solving problems, and following directions (during Homework completion), and joining in, cooperating, problem solving, keeping a good attitude, and following directions (during free play).

Collect Homework and the bottom half of Home Notes; oversee free play and Homework completion or practice time.

Teacher 1:
(Scan papers to see which children have satisfactorily completed Homework; put aside Home Notes to check later.)

(children who completed it), you may go now and choose a game to play. (children who have not completed it), it's time for you to finish the Homework (or practice the skill) so that you can join the others.

(For children who habitually do not bring completed Homework, add more written questions or role play practice so that they finish about the same time as free play ends.)

Review Homework with children.

Teacher 1:
(Have children form a circle on the floor.)

Now let's look at the Homework you have done. I'm glad that (children who brought completed work) did their work at home. (a child who brought it), will you read your answer to Question _____?

(Have several children who brought their work read answers; ask for feedback from others. If you are using the Homework Progress Chart, allow children to color in the whole square or place a sticker in the square or color in part of it, depending on whether they brought completed Homework or finished it during free play.)

---

*Relaxation Training

In addition to today's skill and children's individual target behaviors, give special attention to keeping a calm body, solving problems, following directions, and keeping hands to self.

Lead relaxation training.

Teacher 1:
We are going to practice relaxing again. Relaxing will help you learn the new skill and help you face any problem.

(Have children find a place on the floor to lie down. Choose one child to turn off the lights.)

(Use Relaxation Script 2.)

Skill Lesson 3

● **Introduce skill and list components.**

Teacher 1:
Today we are going to talk about giving and receiving Positive Feedback. Positive Feedback means saying something good about what the person did. To give Positive Feedback, you:
- Use a pleasant face and voice.
- Look at the person.
- Tell the person exactly what you like about what the person did.
- Tell the person right after it was done.

To receive Positive Feedback, you:
- Use a pleasant face and voice.
- Look at the person.
- Acknowledge the feedback by saying, "thanks" or, "you're welcome."

. . . .

● **Role play appropriate example.**

Teacher 1:
This is the right way to give and receive Positive Feedback. I'm with my dad, and he has just dropped me off at the park.
Thanks, dad; that was nice of you to bring me over here. (eye contact and pleasant face and voice)

Teacher 2:
Sure, you're welcome. (eye contact and pleasant face and voice)

● **Ask children for behavior components of skill.**

Teacher 1:
How did you know that was the right way to give and receive Positive Feedback?
(children respond or are prompted)

● **Role play inappropriate example.**

Teacher 1:
This is the wrong way to give and receive Positive Feedback. I'm with my dad, and he has just dropped me off at the park.
Bye, dad! (no eye contact, but has pleasant face and voice)

Teacher 2:
Bye. (no eye contact)

● **Ask children for behavior components of skill.**

Teacher 1:
What should have happened to make that the right way to give and receive Positive Feedback?

(children respond or are prompted)

. . . .

● **Ask children to role play.**

Teacher 1:
Now it is your turn to role play. (Assign role play situation.) I am going to call on someone who has been working really hard in the group by (specific on-task behaviors). _____ has been working really hard the whole time by (appropriate behaviors) and looks ready to be the first one to role play. _____, this is your role play.

(Describe the role play you have previously selected for this child from the role play sheet behind this session outline. Have each child role play the skill *correctly* at least one time.)

● **Ask children to give Positive Feedback.**

Teacher 1 or 2:
Good role playing. Who can give _____ *some Positive Feedback on his/her role play?*

(Call on child who is volunteering and paying attention.)

. . . .

● **Ask children for rationales for using skill.**

Teacher 1:
Why do you think it is important to give and receive Positive Feedback?
(children respond or are prompted)

Children:
- Makes people feel important/good.
- Makes friends.
- Encourages people to do well more often.
- Makes people happier to do things for you.
- People will compliment you more often when you receive it the right way.

. . . .

● **Lead children through reality check.**

Teacher 1:
Sometimes you might try really hard to give or receive Positive Feedback, *and this might happen.* I'm with my dad and he has just dropped me off at the park.
Thanks, dad; that was nice of you to bring me over here. (eye contact and pleasant face and voice)

Teacher 2:
You'd better thank me! I have a lot of things to do today, and bringing you here messes up my whole schedule!

Teacher 1:
You just did everything right to give Positive Feedback.
What should you do if this happens to you?
(children respond or are prompted)

Children:
- Take a deep breath to get calm.
- Keep a good attitude.
- Thank the person again.
- Ignore.
- Try again later.

---

*Snack Time

In addition to today's skill and children's individual target behaviors, give special attention to following group rules, using conversation skills, cooperating, and solving problems.

Decide which children have earned all of snack.

Children may earn the entire snack or only a smaller portion if they join the snack in progress. Keep in mind how much difficulty a child has had following rules or practicing during the lesson and relaxation time to get an idea of how much time the child might need to practice to compensate for missed opportunities.

Dismiss children who have already earned snack time to the snack table.

Teacher 1:
OK, it's snack time now. (Teacher 2), who do you think has really been earning snack today?

Teacher 2:
Well, _____ has been really following the rules, having a still body, volunteering, and working on (his/her target behavior).

Teacher 1:
Yes, he/she really has. And I think _____ has also done a really good job of (specific behaviors). I'd like (child already named) to go to the snack table and pass out the napkins and (other child named) to go and pass out the cups.

(Continue dismissing children to the snack table by giving Positive Feedback for their accomplishments and assigning them a task at the snack table. If some children have not earned all of snack, have them practice as follows.)

Teacher 1:
_____, you need to sit here with me and practice (volunteering, keeping hands to self, etc.).

(Ask children questions from the lesson, have them role play, or do relaxation to give them opportunities to practice behaviors that were problematic during relaxation and/or the lesson. As the children practice, watch for a good attitude and effort in practicing and determine when each child seems to have made up for lost opportunities and achieved an acceptable level of competence in the skill or rule following.)

Ask children to clean up snack area.

Teacher 1:
OK, snack time is over now. We need to clean up. _____, would you get the garbage can and bring it around so everyone can throw away the garbage.

(Use Positive Feedback and other Teaching Strategies for cooperating and following directions during the cleanup.)

---

*Activity Time

In addition to today's skill and children's individual target behaviors, give special attention to following group rules, using conversation skills, cooperating, and solving problems.

Explain activity for today's lesson.

Teacher 1:
It's time for an activity now. Today we're going to (describe activity briefly). This is a time for us to practice our target behaviors and Giving and Receiving Positive Feedback.

(Use Activity.)

Ask all the children to help clean up.

Teacher 1:
Now it's time for everyone to help clean up.

(Use Positive Feedback and other Teaching Strategies to help children work well together on cleanup. After cleanup, prompt children to return to circle.)

---

*Home Notes

In addition to today's skill and children's individual target behaviors, give special attention to following group rules and saying nice things.

Divide children into two groups and work on scoring Home Notes.

Teacher 1:
(a child), we are going to talk about how you did during today's session. Who can give (that child) some Positive Feedback and tell him/her good things about how he/she did on (target behavior)?

(Score the top half of the Home Note while the children are giving Positive Feedback. Ask for specific feedback for each of the child's target behaviors and add to it with comments you want to make, pointing out progress and areas needing improvement.)

(same child), now what do you think was the best thing you did in group today?
(child responds or is prompted)

Teacher 1:
That's good.

(Add specific descriptions of strong points.)

You might also try to (suggestions for improvement). Here is your Home Note.

(Repeat sequence with each child.)

---

*New Homework

In addition to today's skill and children's individual target behaviors, give special attention to following group rules and saying nice things.

Pass out Homework.

Teacher 1:
Here is your Homework. Be sure to do it and bring it back next time. Let's see what it says.

(Read aloud.)

If you need help, ask your parents or some other adult in your home.

Relaxation Script 2

(This script may be used in conjunction with Skills 3, 4, and 5. Please review the section on relaxation training in Chapter 5 of the Guide.)

Today we'll be practicing how to relax each part of our bodies. Think back about how good your body felt when your muscles were calm and relaxed; as I count to three, breathe in slowly, and as you breathe out, *think* the words "I AM CALM" to yourself. (count aloud slowly) One . . . two . . . three. Hold it. (pause) Let it go. (pause) One more time. Breathe in . . . and hold. (pause) Relax.

Now that your stomach feels more relaxed, let's concentrate on the rest of your body. Make your face tense by closing your eyes and mouth tightly and by wrinkling your forehead. Hold it. (count aloud slowly) One . . . two . . . three. Now let your face go loose. (pause) As I count to three, breathe in slowly, and as you breathe out, think the words "I AM CALM." (count aloud slowly) One . . . two . . . three. (pause) Relax. Feel your face relaxing. (pause) Keeping the rest of your body relaxed, tighten just your shoulders. Try to push both your shoulder blades through the floor. Hold it. (count aloud slowly) One . . . two . . . three. Now let your shoulders go loose. (pause) As I count to three, breathe in slowly, and as you breathe out, think the words "I AM CALM." (count aloud slowly) One . . . two . . . three. (pause) Relax.

Keeping your face and shoulders relaxed, tighten only your arms and hands. Make your hands into fists and try to push both your arms through the floor. (pause) Make your muscles feel tight and tense. Hold it. (count aloud slowly) One . . . two . . . three. Let your arms and hands relax. (pause) As I count to three, breathe in slowly, and as you breathe out, think the words "I AM CALM." (count aloud slowly) One . . . two . . . three. (pause) Relax. It feels so much better when you can keep your body relaxed.

Now that your face, shoulders, arms, and hands are calm, let's make your stomach feel relaxed, too. Make your stomach as skinny as you can; try to make your stomach touch your back. Your stomach feels tense and tight. Hold it. (count aloud slowly) One . . . two . . . three. Now relax; let your stomach go soft. (pause) As I count to three, breathe in slowly, and as you breathe out, think the words "I AM CALM." (count aloud slowly) One . . . two . . . three. (pause) Relax.

Keeping the rest of your body relaxed, tighten just your leg muscles. Try pushing your bottom, your legs, and your feet through the floor. Hold it. (count aloud slowly) One . . . two . . . three. Now let your legs go loose. (pause) As I count to three, breathe in slowly, and as you breathe out, think the words "I AM CALM." (count aloud slowly) One . . . two . . . three. Relax.

Now your whole body feels calm, relaxed, and still. All the muscles in your face, shoulders, arms, stomach, and legs feel soft and loose. (pause) As I count to three, breathe in slowly, and as you breathe out, think the words "I AM CALM." (count aloud slowly) One . . . two . . . three. (pause) Relax.

Now that your body is calm, I want you to imagine yourself at home. Your mom is feeling angry; she is slamming pots and pans around the kitchen. Or perhaps you are working with your dad in the garage, and he begins to throw tools around; he gets an angry frown on his face. You feel nervous; you wonder if you did something wrong. What should you do now? Your stomach feels tense. Tighten the parts of your body that are upset; maybe your stomach, arms, and face. Hold it. (count aloud slowly) One . . . two . . . three. Now relax them. (pause) As I count to three, breathe in slowly, and as you breathe out, think the words "I AM CALM." (count aloud slowly) One . . . two . . . three. (pause) Relax. Now your body feels relaxed; you can stay calm when someone around you is angry. (pause) One more time, think about being with someone who is feeling angry, but this time keep your body calm and relaxed. (pause) As I count to three, breathe in slowly, and as you breathe out, think the words "I AM CALM." (count aloud slowly) One . . . two . . . three. (pause) Relax. You feel so much better when you can keep your body calm.

Now I want you to think of another time when you were feeling uncomfortable because someone else around you was feeling angry or sad. (pause and give children a chance to think of their own situations) Imagine yourself in this situation and with those people. Your stomach feels upset; your arms and face feel tense. Tighten the parts of your body that feel uncomfortable. Hold it. (count aloud slowly) One . . . two . . . three. Now relax them. (pause) As I count to three, breathe in slowly, and as you breathe out, think the words "I AM CALM." (count aloud slowly) One . . . two . . . three. (pause) Relax.

One more time, think about being with someone who is feeling angry or sad, but this time keep your body calm and relaxed. (pause) As I count to three, breathe in slowly, and as you breathe out, think the words "I AM CALM." (count aloud slowly) One . . . two . . . three. (pause) Relax. Now each time someone else is angry or sad you can stay calm and relaxed.

Skill 3: Giving and Receiving Positive Feedback
Role Plays

Situations Target Behaviors	School Problems (Teacher/Peers)	Neighborhood Problems	Sibling Problems	Parent Problems
Listen Carefully	You forgot what the math assignment is for tomorrow. Your teacher offers to help you write it down.	Your friend tells you all about his vacation to Disneyland. You have been wanting to hear about it for a long time.	Your older sister reads you a story out of a new book she just got.	Your dad reads you two bedtime stories instead of just one tonight.
Treat Others Nicely	A new kid at school saw you waiting for the swing and gets off so you can have a turn.	A little neighbor kid who is usually a pest helps you rake the lawn and water the flowers.	Your little brother bumps you and causes you to drop your ice cream. He offers to share his with you.	Your mom stops reading the newspaper to help you with your homework.
Join in with Others	The kid who sits next to you in class asks you if you want to join him in an art project he is doing.	Some older kids who live next door to you ask you if you want to play in the park with them.	Your older brothers ask you to play soccer with them and their friends.	Your parents ask you if you want to play bingo with them after dinner.
Keep a Good Attitude	You lost your homework on the way to school. A kid finds it and brings it to your classroom.	You are getting paid to take care of the neighbor's cat. When the cat runs away, a friend offers to help find it.	You haven't done your chores yet today. Your sister offers to help you do them quickly before your parents get home.	You forgot that your dad told you to clean up the garage. Your mom helps you do it before your dad comes home.
Take Responsibility for Self	Someone stole your new crayons out of your desk. A friend offers to share hers with you.	The kids you like to play with have gone to the park without you. A little neighbor girl invites you to her house.	You can't find your favorite tee shirt to wear to school today. Your older brother lets you choose one of his to wear.	Your parents decide that you can't play outside after dinner. But your mom lets you stay up ½ hour longer tonight.
Stay Calm and Relaxed	You are having a spelling test today that you did not know about. A friend offers to help you study at recess time.	After you sweep the drive, a kid throws sand on it. A friend helps you sweep it one more time.	When you get to the store, you see that you don't have as much money as you need for some gum. Your sister loans you a dime.	Your mom gave you some hard chores to do today. Your dad helps you wash the windows you can't reach.
Solve Problems	You can't find your lunch money. The kid next to you in the cafeteria offers to share his sandwich with you.	Some older kids you like ask you to go swimming with them. You want to go but have to stay home and babysit.	You get your new boots muddy. Your brother helps you clean them up before you get home.	You want to go to your friend's house, but it is too far to walk. Your dad offers to give you a ride.

Skill 3: Giving and Receiving Positive Feedback
Activity

(The activity provided for Skill 9: Sharing can also be used here with Skill 3.)

The materials needed are:

1. Paints, crayons, or markers for each group of children.
2. A large sheet of butcher paper for each group of children.

Children should be in groups of four to six. If you have eight or more children, you may want to split them into more than one group.

Tell the children that you want them to paint their neighborhood. Each child should have one color and one job to do. Thus, the person with the black paint would paint the roads while the person with green paint would make grass and trees, the one with brown paint would be in charge of making houses, etc. However, jobs and colors can be traded. The children don't have to stay with one color and one job but can trade off. They should be encouraged to work together to decide where everything should go in their neighborhood.

Point out and praise spontaneous occurrences of Giving and Receiving Positive Feedback, such as "You did a good job on that house," "Thanks for trading jobs with me," or "That's a good idea."

If a child does not spontaneously use Positive Feedback, take aside a child working next to him/her and prompt that child to do something nice for the target child. If necessary, use the Direct Prompt or Teaching Interaction to help the children give and receive Positive Feedback. You as teachers can also participate in the activity and model examples of Giving and Receiving Positive Feedback.

Skill 3: Giving and Receiving Positive Feedback
Home Note

Name _____ Instructors _____

During today's lesson we practiced giving Positive Feedback to someone when he/she does something we like and receiving Positive Feedback when someone says something nice about what we did.

Today's Objectives	Target Behaviors

Today's Objectives

To give Positive Feedback, did the child:

	YES	NO
1. Use a pleasant face and voice?	____	____
2. Look at the person?	____	____
3. Tell the person exactly what he/she liked about what the person did?	____	____
4. Tell the person right after it was done?	____	____

To receive Positive Feedback, did the child:

	YES	NO
5. Use a pleasant face and voice?	____	____
6. Look at the person?	____	____
7. Acknowledge the feedback by saying, "Thanks" or, "You're welcome"?	____	____

Target Behaviors

Score

A. _____ _____
B. _____ _____
C. _____ _____
D. _____ _____
E. _____ _____

Score, using this scale:
1 = Completely satisfied
2 = Satisfied
3 = Slightly satisfied
4 = Neither satisfied nor dissatisfied
5 = Slightly dissatisfied
6 = Dissatisfied
7 = Completely dissatisfied

The best thing your child did today in social skills was _____

_____

- -

Parents – Please Complete This Section and Return
Skill 3: Giving and Receiving Positive Feedback

Name _____

The following objectives and target behaviors refer to those named above. Please mark or score your child in these areas and have him/her return this bottom section with your signature to the next social skills group.

Did your child meet the objectives of today's lesson at least once this week?

	YES	NO
Objective 1	____	____
Objective 2	____	____
Objective 3	____	____
Objective 4	____	____
Objective 5	____	____
Objective 6	____	____
Objective 7	____	____

Score your child on his/her target behaviors, using the 1-7 scale above:

Target Behavior A _____

Target Behavior B _____

Target Behavior C _____

Target Behavior D _____

Target Behavior E _____

Parent Signature _____ Date _____

Skill 3: Giving and Receiving Positive Feedback
Homework

Name _____

1. Give some Positive Feedback to your mom or dad. Write down exactly what you said and what your mom or dad said and did.

   a. What did you say? _____

   _____

   b. What did your mom or dad say and do?_____

   _____

2. Give some Positive Feedback to a friend or one of your brothers or sisters. Write down exactly what you said and what the other person said and did.

   a. What did you say? _____

   _____

   b. What did the other person say and do?_____

   _____

3. Write down some Positive Feedback that someone gave to you. Write down exactly what they said and what you said and did.

   a. What did the other person say? _____

   _____

   b. What did you say and do? _____

   _____

4. Why is it important to thank someone for giving you Positive Feedback?

   a. _____

   _____

   b. _____

   _____

   c. _____

   _____

   d. _____

   _____

Session 4

Skill 4: Sending an "I'm Interested" Message

YOU MAY SUBSTITUTE naturally occurring events (lunch time, art projects, etc.) for items marked with an asterisk. Be sure to incidentally teach the day's skill, target behaviors, and the behaviors listed whether you use these activities or others. Remember that the dialogue provided in the session outlines (except for the lesson itself) is intended to be a model, not read or memorized verbatim. Read the dialogue over for main points and use your own spontaneous style. **Most of the dialogue and instructions are identical from skill to skill. For efficiency you may wish to attend only to the Relaxation Script number and the new information in the Skill Lesson.**

---

*Homework Completion and Free Play

In addition to today's skill and children's individual target behaviors, give special attention to taking responsibility, solving problems, and following directions (during Homework completion), and joining in, cooperating, problem solving, keeping a good attitude, and following directions (during free play).

Collect Homework and the bottom half of Home Notes; oversee free play and Homework completion or practice time.

Teacher 1:

(Scan papers to see which children have satisfactorily completed Homework; put aside Home Notes to check later.)

(children who completed it), you may go now and choose a game to play. (children who have not completed it), it's time for you to finish the Homework (or practice the skill) so that you can join the others.

(For children who habitually do not bring completed Homework, add more written questions or role play practice so that they finish about the same time as free play ends.)

Review Homework with children.

Teacher 1:
(Have children form a circle on the floor.)

Now let's look at the Homework you have done. I'm glad that (children who brought completed work) did their work at home. (a child who brought it), will you read your answer to Question _____?

(Have several children who brought their work read answers; ask for feedback from others. If you are using the Homework Progress Chart, allow children to color in the whole square or place a sticker in the square or color in part of it, depending on whether they brought completed Homework or finished it during free play.)

---

*Relaxation Training

In addition to today's skill and children's individual target behaviors, give special attention to keeping a calm body, solving problems, following directions, and keeping hands to self.

Lead relaxation training.

Teacher 1:
We are going to practice relaxing again. Relaxing will help you learn the new skill and help you face any problem.

(Have children find a place on the floor to lie down. Choose one child to turn off the lights.)

(Use Relaxation Script 2.)

Skill Lesson 4

● Introduce skill and list components.

Teacher 1:
Today we are going to talk about sending "I'm interested"
messages. When you want to show someone you are
interested in what he/she is saying or doing, you send
an "I'm interested" message. To send an "I'm
interested" message, you:
- Use a pleasant face.
- Look at the person.
- Keep your hands and body still.

. . . .

● Role play appropriate example.

Teacher 1:
This is the right way to send an "I'm interested" message.
I'm at school and my teacher is about to give some
directions.

Teacher 1:
(looks at Teacher 2 with a pleasant face and keeps
hands and body still)

Teacher 2:
Today everyone needs to finish all the even-numbered
problems on pages 52 and 53 of your math book.

● Ask children for behavior components of skill.

Teacher 1:
How did you know that was the right way to send an "I'm
interested" message?
(children respond or are prompted)

● Role play inappropriate example.

Teacher 1:
This is the wrong way to send an "I'm interested" message. I'm at school, and my teacher is about to give
some directions.

Teacher 1:
(doesn't look at Teacher 2, plays with pencil, opens up
desk)

Teacher 2:
Today everyone needs to finish all the even-numbered
problems on pages 52 and 53 of your math book.

● Ask children for behavior components of skill.

Teacher 1:
What should have happened to make that the right way to
send an "I'm interested" message?

(children respond or are prompted)
. . . .

● Ask children to role play.

Teacher 1:
Now it is your turn to role play. (Assign role play situation.) I am going to call on someone who has been
working really hard in the group by (specific on-task behaviors).
_____ has been working really hard the
whole time by (appropriate behaviors) and looks ready to be
the first one to role play. _____, this is your
role play.

(Describe the role play you have previously selected for
this child from the role play sheet behind this session
outline. Have each child role play the skill *correctly* at
least one time.)

● Ask children to give Positive Feedback.

Teacher 1 or 2:
Good role playing. Who can give _____ *some
Positive Feedback on his/her role play?*

(Call on child who is volunteering and paying
attention.)
. . . .

● Ask children for rationales for using skill.

Teacher 1:
Why do you think it is important to send "I'm interested"
messages?
(children respond or are prompted)

Children:
- People like you if you show you like them.
- Teachers and parents know you are listening.
- You'll seem friendlier to others.
- Directions will be clearer to you.
- People will be more interested in *you.*
. . . .

● Lead children through reality check.

Teacher 1:
Sometimes you might try really hard to send an "I'm
interested" message, *and this might happen.* I'm at
school, and my teacher is about to give some directions.

Teacher 1:
(looks at Teacher 2 with a pleasant face and keeps
hands and body still)

Teacher 2:
Today everyone needs to finish all the even-numbered
problems on pages 52 and 53 of your math book.
(pause) Since no one was paying attention just then,
everyone has to do an extra page of math!

Teacher 1:
You just did everything right to send an "I'm interested" message. *What should you do if this happens to you?* (children respond or are prompted)

Children:
- Take a deep breath to get calm.
- Keep a good attitude.
- Keep showing interest.
- Do the assignment.

---

*Snack Time

In addition to today's skill and children's individual target behaviors, give special attention to following group rules, using conversation skills, cooperating, and solving problems.

Decide which children have earned all of snack.

Children may earn the entire snack or only a smaller portion if they join the snack in progress. Keep in mind how much difficulty a child has had following rules or practicing during the lesson and relaxation time to get an idea of how much time the child might need to practice to compensate for missed opportunities.

Dismiss children who have already earned snack time to the snack table.

Teacher 1:
OK, it's snack time now. (Teacher 2), who do you think has really been earning snack today?

Teacher 2:
Well, _____ has been really following the rules, having a still body, volunteering, and working on (his/her target behavior).

Teacher 1:
Yes, he/she really has. And I think _____ has also done a really good job of (specific behaviors). I'd like (child already named) to go to the snack table and pass out the napkins and (other child named) to go and pass out the cups.

(Continue dismissing children to the snack table by giving Positive Feedback for their accomplishments and assigning them a task at the snack table. If some children have not earned all of snack, have them practice as follows.)

Teacher 1:
_____, you need to sit here with me and practice (volunteering, keeping hands to self, etc.).

(Ask children questions from the lesson, have them role play, or do relaxation to give them opportunities to practice behaviors that were problematic during relaxation and/or the lesson. As the children practice, watch for a good attitude and effort in practicing and determine when each child seems to have made up for lost opportunities and achieved an acceptable level of competence in the skill or rule following.)

Ask children to clean up snack area.

Teacher 1:
OK, snack time is over now. We need to clean up. _____, would you get the garbage can and bring it around so everyone can throw away the garbage.

(Use Positive Feedback and other Teaching Strategies for cooperating and following directions during the cleanup.)

---

*Activity Time

In addition to today's skill and children's individual target behaviors, give special attention to following group rules, using conversation skills, cooperating, and solving problems.

Explain activity for today's lesson.

Teacher 1:
It's time for an activity now. Today we're going to (describe activity briefly). This is a time for us to practice our target behaviors and Sending an "I'm Interested" Message.

(Use Activity.)

Ask all the children to help clean up.

Teacher 1:
Now it's time for everyone to help clean up.

(Use Positive Feedback and other Teaching Strategies to help children work well together on cleanup. After cleanup, prompt children to return to circle.)

---

*Home Notes

In addition to today's skill and children's individual target behaviors, give special attention to following group rules and saying nice things.

Divide children into two groups and work on scoring Home Notes.

Teacher 1:
(a child), we are going to talk about how you did during today's session. Who can give (that child) some Positive Feedback and tell him/her good things about how he/she did on (target behavior)?

(Score the top half of the Home Note while the children are giving Positive Feedback. Ask for specific feedback for each of the child's target behaviors and add to it with comments you want to make, pointing out progress and areas needing improvement.)

(same child), now what do you think was the best thing you did in group today?
(child responds or is prompted)

Teacher 1:
That's good.

(Add specific descriptions of strong points.)

You might also try to (suggestions for improvement). Here is your Home Note.

(Repeat sequence with each child.)

---

*New Homework

In addition to today's skill and children's individual target behaviors, give special attention to following group rules and saying nice things.

Pass out Homework.

Teacher 1:
Here is your Homework. Be sure to do it and bring it back next time. Let's see what it says.

(Read aloud.)

If you need help, ask your parents or some other adult in your home.

Skill 4: Sending an "I'm Interested" Message
Role Plays

Situations Target Behaviors	School Problems (Teacher/Peers)	Neighborhood Problems	Sibling Problems	Parent Problems
Listen Carefully	Your teacher is telling what your spelling homework is for tomorrow.	You're at your friend's house. His mom is telling you how to make dessert.	Your sister is telling you about an exciting movie she saw last night.	Your dad is telling about the fish he caught this afternoon.
Treat Others Nicely	A little first-grader is telling you how she hit a home run in a softball game.	A friend whom you like to play with is telling you the rules to a new game. You already know how to play this game.	Your little brother is telling you a riddle he heard at school today.	Your mom is telling you about what a hard day she had at work.
Join in with Others	Two of your friends are talking about soccer, which is your very favorite sport.	Your friend is telling a ghost story that you've never heard before.	Your sisters are talking about all the fun they are going to have at summer camp this year.	Your parents are deciding where the family will go on vacation this year.
Keep a Good Attitude	A friend is helping you finish some math problems that you didn't know how to do.	Your neighbor is going to pay you to do some yard work. He is telling you what needs to be done.	Your older brother is babysitting you. He is telling you what chores your mom wanted you to do.	Your mom is giving you some new chores to do. They must be done right before you can go to the park.
Take Responsibility for Self	Your teacher is giving you all of the assignments that you missed while you were absent from school.	You had to do chores today and didn't get to go to the park with your friend. She is telling you about all of the things she did.	You didn't get to go to the movies with your sister, but she is telling all about them.	Your dad is explaining to you how you have to do all of your math homework over because you have done it all wrong.
Stay Calm and Relaxed	The principal is telling your class what is going to happen to the next kid he sees throwing sand on the playground.	Your dog walked on the neighbor's flowers. She is telling you how she wants you to clean up the flower bed.	You've asked to play with some of your brother's birthday toys. He is telling you how he wants them to be put away.	It's your turn to clean up the kitchen. Your dad is explaining to you how to load the dishwasher.
Solve Problems	You forgot your lunch money today. Your teacher is explaining to you how to charge your lunch in the cafeteria.	You missed your ride to the park. Your friend is explaining to you how to get to the park by walking.	You've lost the map to your friend's house. Your sister is explaining how to get there.	Your mom is telling you what to get at the store. The list is really long.

Skill 4: Sending an "I'm Interested" Message
Activity

The materials needed are:

1. Old clothes, hats, wigs, and other "dress-up" accessories (optional).
2. Prizes such as small cups of trail mix, stickers, or, if possible, a Polaroid camera and film to take pictures of the children that they might win and take home.

Have the children divide into groups of two and discuss a T.V. show or movie they will want to portray in their charades. Limit this discussion to 2 minutes; use a timer if available. You may want to give the children lists of T.V. shows or movies to expedite the process. Once they have decided on a theme, allow them to choose costumes from the old clothes. (This is optional; you may prefer to do the activity without costumes.) This should also be time limited. When the children are prepared, have them present their charades to the group. The audience is to send "I'm interested" messages throughout the performances.

An optional feature of the activity is the use of points for those sending "I'm interested" messages. Members of the audience could earn 1 or 2 points for listening quietly and looking at the speaker. Remind the children that they can still earn points after they have had their turn.

Throughout the activity, be contingent with the privilege of proceeding to the next step. Be particularly concerned with quiet mouths and looking at the speaker.

Skill 4: Sending an "I'm Interested" Message
Optional Activity

The materials needed are:

1. A pencil for each child.
2. A piece of paper for each child.

Have each child write down two incidents from the past week that she/he felt really good about and two that she/he would have liked to improve. Instruct the children to use incidents that had to do with how they got along with another person. Go around the circle taking turns; each child will choose one of her/his incidents to describe to the group. Other members of the group will send "I'm interested" messages to the speaker. The speaker will then give members of the group Positive Feedback for their "I'm interested" messages. Continue until everyone has had a chance to do all four incidents. You may want to do this in two small groups and participate with the children.

Skill 4: Sending an "I'm Interested" Message
Home Note

Name _____ Instructors _____

During today's lesson we practiced sending an "I'm interested" message to a person who is talking, in order to let the person know we're listening and paying attention.

Today's Objectives			**Target Behaviors**	
To send an "I'm interested" message, did the child:				Score
	YES	NO	A. _____	_____
1. Use a pleasant face?	_____	_____	B. _____	_____
2. Look at the person?	_____	_____	C. _____	_____
3. Keep hands and body still?	_____	_____	D. _____	_____
			E. _____	_____

Score, using this scale:
1 = Completely satisfied
2 = Satisfied
3 = Slightly satisfied
4 = Neither satisfied nor dissatisfied
5 = Slightly dissatisfied
6 = Dissatisfied
7 = Completely dissatisfied

The best thing your child did today in social skills was _____
_____

- -

Parents – Please Complete This Section and Return
Skill 4: Sending an "I'm Interested" Message

Name _____

The following objectives and target behaviors refer to those named above. Please mark or score your child in these areas and have him/her return this bottom section with your signature to the next social skills group.

Did your child meet the objectives of today's lesson at least once this week?			
	YES	NO	Score your child on his/her target behaviors, using the 1-7 scale above:
Objective 1	_____	_____	Target Behavior A _____
Objective 2	_____	_____	Target Behavior B _____
Objective 3	_____	_____	Target Behavior C _____
			Target Behavior D _____
			Target Behavior E _____

Parent Signature _____ Date _____

Skill 4: Sending an "I'm Interested" Message
Homework

Name _____

1. Ask your mom or dad if you may borrow a magazine or newspaper so that you can cut out pictures. In the boxes below paste a picture of someone feeling happy, tired, sad, and calm (if you do not have magazines or newspapers, you may draw the pictures).

Happy

Tired

Sad

Calm

2. Draw a circle around the person(s) you would like to play with. *Why* did you choose that person/those people?

_____

_____

_____

3. Find or draw a picture of two people who look interested in each other and paste it on the back of this paper. List two ways you can tell they are interested in each other.

a. _____

_____

b. _____

_____

Session 5

Skill 5: Sending an Ignoring Message

YOU MAY SUBSTITUTE naturally occurring events (lunch time, art projects, etc.) for items marked with an asterisk. Be sure to incidentally teach the day's skill, target behaviors, and the behaviors listed whether you use these activities or others. Remember that the dialogue provided in the session outlines (except for the lesson itself) is intended to be a model, not read or memorized verbatim. Read the dialogue over for main points and use your own spontaneous style. **Most of the dialogue and instructions are identical from skill to skill. For efficiency you may wish to attend only to the Relaxation Script number and the new information in the Skill Lesson.**

---

*Homework Completion and Free Play

In addition to today's skill and children's individual target behaviors, give special attention to taking responsibility, solving problems, and following directions (during Homework completion), and joining in, cooperating, problem solving, keeping a good attitude, and following directions (during free play).

Collect Homework and the bottom half of Home Notes; oversee free play and Homework completion or practice time.

Teacher 1:
(Scan papers to see which children have satisfactorily completed Homework; put aside Home Notes to check later.)

(children who completed it), you may go now and choose a game to play. (children who have not completed it), it's time for you to finish the Homework (or practice the skill) so that you can join the others.

(For children who habitually do not bring completed Homework, add more written questions or role play practice so that they finish about the same time as free play ends.)

Review Homework with children.

Teacher 1:
(Have children form a circle on the floor.)

Now let's look at the Homework you have done. I'm glad that (children who brought completed work) did their work at home. (a child who brought it), will you read your answer to Question _____?

(Have several children who brought their work read answers; ask for feedback from others. If you are using the Homework Progress Chart, allow children to color in the whole square or place a sticker in the square or color in part of it, depending on whether they brought completed Homework or finished it during free play.)

---

*Relaxation Training

In addition to today's skill and children's individual target behaviors, give special attention to keeping a calm body, solving problems, following directions, and keeping hands to self.

Lead relaxation training.

Teacher 1:
We are going to practice relaxing again. Relaxing will help you learn the new skill and help you face any problem.

(Have children find a place on the floor to lie down. Choose one child to turn off the lights.)

(Use Relaxation Script 2.)

41

Skill Lesson 5

● **Introduce skill and list components.**

Teacher 1:
Today we are going to talk about sending an ignoring message. When you want to show someone that you are not interested in what a person is saying or doing, you send an ignoring message. To send an ignoring message, you:
- Keep a pleasant face.
- Look away or walk away from the person.
- Keep a quiet mouth.
- Pretend you're not listening.

. . . .

● **Role play appropriate example.**

Teacher 1:
This is the right way to send an ignoring message. I'm in class, and my friend wants to talk during math. I need to do my math. (keeps eyes on math during entire role play)

Teacher 2:
(taps Teacher 1 on the shoulder repeatedly) Hey, _____. Pssst! (eventually quits)

● **Ask children for behavior components of skill.**

Teacher 1:
How did you know that was the right way to send an ignoring message?
(children respond or are prompted)

● **Role play inappropriate example.**

Teacher 1:
This is the wrong way to send an ignoring message. I'm in class, and my friend wants to talk during math. I need to do my math. (keeps eyes on math)

Teacher 2:
(taps Teacher 1 on the shoulder repeatedly) Hey, _____. Pssst!

Teacher 1:
Sh-sh. Leave me alone. I'm trying to work.

● **Ask children for behavior components of skill.**

Teacher 1:
What should have happened to make that the right way to send an ignoring message?

(children respond or are prompted)

. . . .

● **Ask children to role play.**

Teacher 1:
Now it is your turn to role play. (Assign role play situation.) I am going to call on someone who has been working really hard in the group by (specific on-task behaviors). _____ has been working really hard the whole time by (appropriate behaviors) and looks ready to be the first one to role play. _____, this is your role play.

(Describe the role play you have previously selected for this child from the role play sheet behind this session outline. Have each child role play the skill *correctly* at least one time.)

● **Ask children to give Positive Feedback.**

Teacher 1 or 2:
Good role playing. Who can give _____ *some Positive Feedback on his/her role play?*

(Call on child who is volunteering and paying attention.)

. . . .

● **Ask children for rationales for using skill.**

Teacher 1:
Why do you think it is important to send an ignoring message?
(children respond or are prompted)

Children:
- To keep out of trouble.
- If their attempts to bother you don't work, they'll probably quit trying.

. . . .

● **Lead children through reality check.**

Teacher 1:
Sometimes you might try really hard to send an ignoring message, *and this might happen.* I'm in class, and my friend wants to talk during math. I need to do my work. (keeps eyes on math)

Teacher 2:
(taps Teacher 1 on the shoulder repeatedly) Hey, _____. Pssst!

Teacher 1:
(ignores the right way)

Teacher 2:	Children:
(continues heckling)	• Take a deep breath to get calm.
	• Keep a good attitude.
Teacher 1:	• Keep ignoring.
You just did everything right to send an ignoring message.	• Keep working.
What should you do if this happens to you?	• Keep quiet.
(children respond or are prompted)	

---

*Snack Time

In addition to today's skill and children's individual target behaviors, give special attention to following group rules, using conversation skills, cooperating, and solving problems.

Decide which children have earned all of snack.

Children may earn the entire snack or only a smaller portion if they join the snack in progress. Keep in mind how much difficulty a child has had following rules or practicing during the lesson and relaxation time to get an idea of how much time the child might need to practice to compensate for missed opportunities.

Dismiss children who have already earned snack time to the snack table.

Teacher 1:
OK, it's snack time now. (Teacher 2), who do you think has really been earning snack today?

Teacher 2:
Well, _____ has been really following the rules, having a still body, volunteering, and working on (his/her target behavior).

Teacher 1:
Yes, he/she really has. And I think _____ has also done a really good job of (specific behaviors). I'd like (child already named) to go to the snack table and pass out the napkins and (other child named) to go and pass out the cups.

(Continue dismissing children to the snack table by giving Positive Feedback for their accomplishments and assigning them a task at the snack table. If some children have not earned all of snack, have them practice as follows.)

Teacher 1:
_____, you need to sit here with me and practice (volunteering, keeping hands to self, etc.).

(Ask children questions from the lesson, have them role play, or do relaxation to give them opportunities to practice behaviors that were problematic during relaxation and/or the lesson. As the children practice, watch for a good attitude and effort in practicing and determine when each child seems to have made up for lost opportunities and achieved an acceptable level of competence in the skill or rule following.)

Ask children to clean up snack area.

Teacher 1:
OK, snack time is over now. We need to clean up. _____, would you get the garbage can and bring it around so everyone can throw away the garbage.

(Use Positive Feedback and other Teaching Strategies for cooperating and following directions during the cleanup.)

---

*Activity Time

In addition to today's skill and children's individual target behaviors, give special attention to following group rules, using conversation skills, cooperating, and solving problems.

Explain activity for today's lesson.

Teacher 1:

It's time for an activity now. Today we're going to (describe activity briefly). This is a time for us to practice our target behaviors and Sending an Ignoring Message.

(Use Activity.)

Ask all the children to help clean up.

Teacher 1:

Now it's time for everyone to help clean up.

(Use Positive Feedback and other Teaching Strategies to help children work well together on cleanup. After cleanup, prompt children to return to circle.)

---

*Home Notes

In addition to today's skill and children's individual target behaviors, give special attention to following group rules and saying nice things.

Divide children into two groups and work on scoring Home Notes.

Teacher 1:

(a child), we are going to talk about how you did during today's session. Who can give (that child) some Positive Feedback and tell him/her good things about how he/she did on (target behavior)?

(Score the top half of the Home Note while the children are giving Positive Feedback. Ask for specific feedback for each of the child's target behaviors and add to it with comments you want to make, pointing out progress and areas needing improvement.)

(same child), now what do you think was the best thing you did in group today?
(child responds or is prompted)

Teacher 1:

That's good.

(Add specific descriptions of strong points.)

You might also try to (suggestions for improvement). Here is your Home Note.

(Repeat sequence with each child.)

---

*New Homework

In addition to today's skill and children's individual target behaviors, give special attention to following group rules and saying nice things.

Pass out Homework.

Teacher 1:

Here is your Homework. Be sure to do it and bring it back next time. Let's see what it says.

(Read aloud.)

If you need help, ask your parents or some other adult in your home.

Skill 5: Sending an Ignoring Message
Role Plays

Situations / Target Behaviors	School Problems (Teacher/Peers)	Neighborhood Problems	Sibling Problems	Parent Problems
Listen Carefully	Your teacher says to stay in your seats and read quietly; she leaves the room. Some kids start throwing spit wads.	You're taking a phone message for your mom. Your best friend comes in and starts showing you her brand new toy.	You and your sister are talking. Your baby brother is fussing and whining to get your attention.	Your mom is telling you what your chores are. The T.V. is on, and you hear your favorite show just starting.
Treat Others Nicely	You are talking with some friends. They begin to say mean things about one of your friends.	You just got braces. You go to the store and see some kids from your neighborhood. They start laughing at you.	You're talking on the phone. Your brother comes in. He starts making faces at you and teasing you.	Your mother is complaining to you about how lazy your dad is because he hasn't fixed the dryer yet.
Join in with Others	Your teacher asks a question to which you know the answer. The boy behind you keeps kicking your chair.	Your neighbor is telling you how to take care of his house while he's out of town. Some kids ride by and yell at you.	You and your friend are talking. Your little sister comes up and interrupts you while you're talking.	Your mother is asking you about your day. Your brother is still mad at her and is crying since he can't go to a friend's.
Keep a Good Attitude	You're in a reading group. Your best friend comes into your class on an errand for his teacher.	You're playing with some friends. A couple of them start telling dirty jokes.	You're in church. During the opening prayer your sister starts hiccuping.	You're doing dishes for mom as a surprise. She's talking to dad on the phone and saying that you haven't done anything all day.
Take Responsibility for Self	Your teacher is giving a lesson. The kid next to you starts giggling, burping, and blowing bubbles with his gum.	You and a friend go to the movies. Your friend starts talking right at a really exciting part.	You're at a baseball game. Your brother keeps bugging you to throw popcorn on the people in the bleachers below you.	You're at home watching T.V. Your mom and dad start having a big argument.
Stay Calm and Relaxed	You are taking a test in class. The person sitting next to you whispers, "What's the answer to Number 4?"	You're playing a game with a friend. Your friend loses, gets angry, and starts swearing.	Your sister is bothering you today. She is following you around and repeating everything you say.	Your dad takes off your record and puts on one of his which you hate, saying how stupid your taste in music is.
Solve Problems	You're sitting in the back of the bus. Some kids around you start bouncing in their seats. The bus driver doesn't allow this.	You're about to go to the movies. The neighbor kid comes over and starts telling you stupid jokes. You need to leave.	You want a Popsicle. Your sister says, "Ha, ha; I took the last one and you can't have it" in a taunting tone of voice.	Your homework is very hard. Mom won't help you. While you're doing it, she says, "You can't do anything by yourself!"

45

Skill 5: Sending an Ignoring Message
Activity

The materials needed are:

1. Small prizes such as gum, stickers, etc.
2. "Message cards" (one per child) with fairly detailed instructions, several jokes, the plot of a movie, etc. The length and complexity of these should be determined by the children's abilities, i.e., they should be challenged in learning the information, but it should not be too difficult.

Divide the children into groups of three to four children each. In each group, assign roles: have one child be storyteller, one be listener, and one or more be hecklers. Give the storyteller a message card. Have the storyteller and the listener sit across from one another.

The heckler(s) may sit on the side. When you say "go," the storyteller reads or paraphrases the message on the card, the heckler(s) try to distract the listener by talking (but no touching or name-calling is allowed), and the listener sends "I'm interested" messages to the storyteller and ignoring messages to the heckler(s). When the storyteller is finished, stop the heckler(s) and have the listener repeat the message to you. Give the listener a point for sending ignoring messages to the heckler(s) and one for repeating the message to your satisfaction. The groups of children may be considered to be teams, combining individual points to compete with the other team and win, or individual children may earn a prize for getting 2 points.

Skill 5: Sending an Ignoring Message
Home Note

Name _____ Instructors _____

During today's lesson we practiced sending an ignoring message to a person who tries to distract us during class or at some other inappropriate time. We also practiced looking away or, if possible, walking away if the person continues to be distracting.

Today's Objectives			Target Behaviors	
To send an ignoring message, did the child:				Score
	YES	NO	A. _____	_____
1. Keep a pleasant face?	____	____	B. _____	_____
2. Look away or walk away from the person?	____	____	C. _____	_____
			D. _____	_____
3. Keep a quiet mouth?	____	____	E. _____	_____
4. Pretend he's/she's not listening?	____	____		

Score, using this scale:
1 = Completely satisfied
2 = Satisfied
3 = Slightly satisfied
4 = Neither satisfied nor dissatisfied
5 = Slightly dissatisfied
6 = Dissatisfied
7 = Completely dissatisfied

The best thing your child did today in social skills was _____

_____

- -

Parents – Please Complete This Section and Return
Skill 5: Sending an Ignoring Message

Name _____

The following objectives and target behaviors refer to those named above. Please mark or score your child in these areas and have him/her return this bottom section with your signature to the next social skills group.

Did your child meet the objectives of today's lesson at least once this week?			Score your child on his/her target behaviors, using the 1-7 scale above:
	YES	NO	
Objective 1	____	____	Target Behavior A _____
Objective 2	____	____	Target Behavior B _____
Objective 3	____	____	Target Behavior C _____
Objective 4	____	____	Target Behavior D _____
			Target Behavior E _____

Parent Signature _____ Date _____

Skill 5: Sending an Ignoring Message
Homework

Name _____

1. List three things you would do to send an ignoring message.

    a. _____
    _____

    b. _____
    _____

    c. _____
    _____

2. Name three examples of times when you would want to send an ignoring message to someone.

    a. _____
    _____

    b. _____
    _____

    c. _____
    _____

3. Describe a time when you sent an ignoring message.

    a. Who or what were you ignoring? _____
    _____

    b. What did you do? _____
    _____

    c. What happened? _____

4. If you send an ignoring message to someone but the person keeps bothering you, what are three things you can do?

    a. _____
    _____

    b. _____
    _____

    c. _____
    _____

Session 6

Skill 6: Interrupting a Conversation

YOU MAY SUBSTITUTE naturally occurring events (lunch time, art projects, etc.) for items marked with an asterisk. Be sure to incidentally teach the day's skill, target behaviors, and the behaviors listed whether you use these activities or others. Remember that the dialogue provided in the session outlines (except for the lesson itself) is intended to be a model, not read or memorized verbatim. Read the dialogue over for main points and use your own spontaneous style. **Most of the dialogue and instructions are identical from skill to skill. For efficiency you may wish to attend only to the Relaxation Script number and the new information in the Skill Lesson.**

*Homework Completion and Free Play

In addition to today's skill and children's individual target behaviors, give special attention to taking responsibility, solving problems, and following directions (during Homework completion), and joining in, cooperating, problem solving, keeping a good attitude, and following directions (during free play).

Collect Homework and the bottom half of Home Notes; oversee free play and Homework completion or practice time.

Teacher 1:
(Scan papers to see which children have satisfactorily completed Homework; put aside Home Notes to check later.)

(children who completed it), you may go now and choose a game to play. (children who have not completed it), it's time for you to finish the Homework (or practice the skill) so that you can join the others.

(For children who habitually do not bring completed Homework, add more written questions or role play practice so that they finish about the same time as free play ends.)

Review Homework with children.

Teacher 1:
(Have children form a circle on the floor.)

Now let's look at the Homework you have done. I'm glad that (children who brought completed work) did their work at home. (a child who brought it), will you read your answer to Question _____?

(Have several children who brought their work read answers; ask for feedback from others. If you are using the Homework Progress Chart, allow children to color in the whole square or place a sticker in the square or color in part of it, depending on whether they brought completed Homework or finished it during free play.)

*Relaxation Training

In addition to today's skill and children's individual target behaviors, give special attention to keeping a calm body, solving problems, following directions, and keeping hands to self.

Lead relaxation training.

Teacher 1:
We are going to practice relaxing again. Relaxing will help you learn the new skill and help you face any problem.

(Have children find a place on the floor to lie down. Choose one child to turn off the lights.)

(Use Relaxation Script 3.)

Skill Lesson 6

● **Introduce skill and list components.**

Teacher 1:
Today we are going to talk about interrupting a conversation. You use this when other people are talking and you need to say something important. To interrupt the right way, you:
▪ Use a pleasant face and voice.
▪ Wait for a pause in the conversation.
▪ Look directly at the person.
▪ Say "excuse me."
▪ Then talk.

. . . .

● **Role play appropriate example.**

Teacher 1:
This is the right way to interrupt a conversation. I'm at home. (Teacher 2) is my grandmother, and _____ will be my brother. My grandmother is talking to my brother about his day at school.

Teacher 2:
(talks with brother while (Teacher 1) waits; there is a pause in the conversation)

Teacher 1:
Excuse me, grandma. Ron is outside and wants to know if I can go to his house.

● **Ask children for behavior components of skill.**

Teacher 1:
How did you know that was the right way to interrupt a conversation?
(children respond or are prompted)

● **Role play inappropriate example.**

Teacher 1:
This is the wrong way to interrupt a conversation. I'm at home. (Teacher 2) is my grandmother, and _____ will be my brother. My grandmother is talking to my brother about his day at school.

Teacher 2:
(talks with brother while (Teacher 1) approaches)

Teacher 1:
(doesn't wait for a pause) Grandma, grandma, can I go over to Ron's house?

● **Ask children for behavior components of skill.**

Teacher 1:
What should have happened to make that the right way to interrupt a conversation?

(children respond or are prompted)

. . . .

● **Ask children to role play.**

Teacher 1:
Now it is your turn to role play. (Assign role play situation.) I am going to call on someone who has been working really hard in the group by (specific on-task behaviors). _____ has been working really hard the whole time by (appropriate behaviors) and looks ready to be the first one to role play. _____, this is your role play.

(Describe the role play you have previously selected for this child from the role play sheet behind this session outline. Have each child role play the skill *correctly* at least one time.)

● **Ask children to give Positive Feedback.**

Teacher 1 or 2:
Good role playing. Who can give _____ *some Positive Feedback on his/her role play?*

(Call on child who is volunteering and paying attention.)

. . . .

● **Ask children for rationales for using skill.**

Teacher 1:
Why do you think it is important to interrupt a conversation the right way?
(children respond or are prompted)

Children:
▪ Helps people communicate better.
▪ People will want to listen to you more often.
▪ People will like you because you're polite.

. . . .

● **Lead children through reality check.**

Teacher 1:
Sometimes you might try really hard to interrupt a conversation the right way, *and this might happen.* I'm at home. (Teacher 2) is my grandmother, and _____ is my brother. My grandmother is talking to my brother about his day at school.

Teacher 2:
(talks with brother while (Teacher 1) waits; there is a pause in the conversation)

Teacher 1:
Excuse me, grandma. Ron is outside and wants to know if I can go to his house.

Teacher 2:
Can't you see that we're talking! You're always interrupting!

Teacher 1:
You just did everything right to interrupt. *What should you do if this happens to you?*

(children respond or are prompted)

Children:
- Take a deep breath to get calm.
- Keep a good attitude.
- Ignore.
- Try again later.

---

*Snack Time

In addition to today's skill and children's individual target behaviors, give special attention to following group rules, using conversation skills, cooperating, and solving problems.

Decide which children have earned all of snack.

Children may earn the entire snack or only a smaller portion if they join the snack in progress. Keep in mind how much difficulty a child has had following rules or practicing during the lesson and relaxation time to get an idea of how much time the child might need to practice to compensate for missed opportunities.

Dismiss children who have already earned snack time to the snack table.

Teacher 1:
OK, it's snack time now. (Teacher 2), who do you think has really been earning snack today?

Teacher 2:
Well, _____ has been really following the rules, having a still body, volunteering, and working on (his/her target behavior).

Teacher 1:
Yes, he/she really has. And I think _____ has also done a really good job of (specific behaviors). I'd like (child already named) to go to the snack table and pass out the napkins and (other child named) to go and pass out the cups.

(Continue dismissing children to the snack table by giving Positive Feedback for their accomplishments and assigning them a task at the snack table. If some children have not earned all of snack, have them practice as follows.)

Teacher 1:
_____, you need to sit here with me and practice (volunteering, keeping hands to self, etc.).

(Ask children questions from the lesson, have them role play, or do relaxation to give them opportunities to practice behaviors that were problematic during relaxation and/or the lesson. As the children practice, watch for a good attitude and effort in practicing and determine when each child seems to have made up for lost opportunities and achieved an acceptable level of competence in the skill or rule following.)

Ask children to clean up snack area.

Teacher 1:
OK, snack time is over now. We need to clean up. _____, would you get the garbage can and bring it around so everyone can throw away the garbage.

(Use Positive Feedback and other Teaching Strategies for cooperating and following directions during the cleanup.)

---

*Activity Time

In addition to today's skill and children's individual target behaviors, give special attention to following group rules, using conversation skills, cooperating, and solving problems.

51

Explain activity for today's lesson.

Teacher 1:
It's time for an activity now. Today we're going to (describe activity briefly). This is a time for us to practice our target behaviors and Interrupting a Conversation.

(Use Activity.)

Ask all the children to help clean up.

Teacher 1:
Now it's time for everyone to help clean up.

(Use Positive Feedback and other Teaching Strategies to help children work well together on cleanup. After cleanup, prompt children to return to circle.)

---

*Home Notes

In addition to today's skill and children's individual target behaviors, give special attention to following group rules and saying nice things.

Divide children into two groups and work on scoring Home Notes.

Teacher 1:
(a child), we are going to talk about how you did during today's session. Who can give (that child) some Positive Feedback and tell him/her good things about how he/she did on (target behavior)?

(Score the top half of the Home Note while the children are giving Positive Feedback. Ask for specific feedback for each of the child's target behaviors and add to it with comments you want to make, pointing out progress and areas needing improvement.)

(same child), now what do you think was the best thing you did in group today?
(child responds or is prompted)

Teacher 1:
That's good.

(Add specific descriptions of strong points.)

You might also try to (suggestions for improvement). Here is your Home Note.

(Repeat sequence with each child.)

---

*New Homework

In addition to today's skill and children's individual target behaviors, give special attention to following group rules and saying nice things.

Pass out Homework.

Teacher 1:
Here is your Homework. Be sure to do it and bring it back next time. Let's see what it says.

(Read aloud.)

If you need help, ask your parents or some other adult in your home.

Relaxation Script 3

(This script may be used in conjunction with Skills 6, 7, and 8. Please review the section on relaxation training in Chapter 5 of the Guide.)

Today and from now on we'll be practicing a new way to make our bodies calm. Together we'll learn how to relax our muscles without making them tight or tense. That way you will be able to relax anywhere, without others noticing.

Before we begin, let's take a slow, deep breath and get our bodies ready to start something new. As I count to three, breathe in slowly; then slowly breathe out and think the words "I AM CALM." (count aloud slowly) One . . . two . . . three. (pause) Relax.

First, I want you to try relaxing your arms, without making them tense. Your arms should be lying on the floor next to your sides. Think about how your arms feel. (pause) If they are feeling tense, let them flop quietly at your sides, making them feel soft and loose. (pause) Now your arms feel relaxed.

Now that your arms feel calm, I want you to try it with the rest of your body. Think about how your face, eyes, mouth, and forehead feel. (pause) If they are feeling tense, relax them. (pause) It feels good to have your forehead smooth, your eyes lightly closed, and your mouth and chin relaxed. (pause) As I count to three, breathe in slowly, and as you breathe out, think the words "I AM CALM." (count aloud slowly) One . . . two . . . three. (pause) Relax.

Think about how your shoulders feel. (pause) If they are feeling tight and tense, relax them. (pause) As I count to three, breathe in slowly, and as you breathe out, think the words "I AM CALM." (count aloud slowly) One . . . two . . . three. (pause) Relax.

Think about how your hands and arms feel. (pause) If they are feeling tense or nervous, relax them. As I count to three, breathe in slowly, and as you breathe out, think the words "I AM CALM." (count aloud slowly) One . . . two . . . three. (pause) Relax. Now your arms, shoulders, and face feel relaxed; your body is calm.

Think about how your stomach feels. (pause) If it feels tight, upset, or nervous, relax. (pause) Now it feels warm and relaxed. As I count to three, breathe in slowly, and as you breathe out, think the words "I AM CALM." (count aloud slowly) One . . . two . . . three. (pause) Relax.

Think about how your legs and feet feel. (pause) If they feel tense or wiggly, relax them. (pause) As I count to three, breathe in slowly, and as you breathe out, think the words "I AM CALM." (count aloud slowly) One . . . two . . . three. (pause) Relax.

Now your whole body feels calm and relaxed. All the muscles in your face, shoulders, arms, stomach, and legs feel soft and loose. As I count to three, breathe in slowly, and as you breathe out, think the words "I AM CALM." (count aloud slowly) One . . . two . . . three. (pause) Relax.

Now that your body is calm, I want you to imagine yourself needing to talk to your mom or teacher about something really important, but she is busy talking with someone else. (pause) You wish she would hurry up; your body feels tense and maybe even angry. Think of the tense muscles, maybe in your face, arms, and stomach, and relax them. (pause) As I count to three, breathe in slowly, and as you breathe out, think the words "I AM CALM." (count aloud slowly) One . . . two . . . three. (pause) Relax. Now your body feels relaxed, and you can wait calmly until there is a pause in the conversation.

Let's try another one. Now I want you to imagine yourself in a place where you don't know anyone. Your body feels nervous and tense. You want to talk to these other people to make some new friends, but your stomach feels like it has a knot tied in it. Think of these tight muscles; maybe your stomach, legs, and arms are tense, and your voice is shaky. Let all your muscles relax. (pause) As I count to three, breathe in slowly, and as you breathe out, think the words "I AM CALM." (count aloud slowly) One . . . two . . . three. (pause) Relax. Now that your body feels calm and relaxed, you'll be able to feel more comfortable and make friends in new places.

Now I want you to think of another time when you were feeling angry or upset waiting for someone or a time when you were around others that you did not know. (pause and give children a chance to think of their own situations) Imagine yourself in this situation. Think about how your stomach feels upset and your face and arms feel tense. (pause) If they are feeling tight, let them go. (pause) It feels good to have your body relaxed. (pause) As I count to three, breathe in slowly, and as you breathe out, think the words "I AM CALM." (count aloud slowly) One . . . two . . . three. (pause) Relax.

Now your body feels calm and relaxed. The next time you begin to feel angry, nervous, or afraid, remember how you feel right now. You can make your body feel calm all the time. When you want to relax, think about your body, take a slow, deep breath, and let go of all the tension. You can handle anything when you are calm.

Skill 6: Interrupting a Conversation
Role Plays

Situations / Target Behaviors	School Problems (Teacher/Peers)	Neighborhood Problems	Sibling Problems	Parent Problems
Listen Carefully	Your teacher is giving the homework assignment to the class. You want to tell her that she forgot to hand out books.	Your two neighbor friends are explaining the rules of a game to you. You need to tell them that you can't play today.	Your older sister begins explaining a math problem to you. There's someone on the phone for her.	Your dad is giving you a list of chores to do. You notice that the dog is digging in the flower garden.
Treat Others Nicely	Two kids are talking in the doorway. You want to get out to recess right away.	Your friends are talking about a swimming class. You want to share some ice cream with them.	Your brothers are complaining that they have nothing to do. You just learned a new game you could teach them.	Your two little cousins are outside talking. Your dad tells you to invite them inside for a soda.
Join in with Others	Two classmates are talking about a movie. You need to tell one that the principal wants to see him.	Your friends are talking about a game they played yesterday. You want to suggest that you all play it right now.	Your older sister and brother are talking about which pizza parlor to go to. You want to suggest a different place.	Your parents are deciding where to go for a vacation this year. You want to suggest Disneyland.
Keep a Good Attitude	Two classmates are bragging about how well they can spell. You can't spell well, but you need a partner for a game.	Your friend's mom is explaining how to make doughnuts. But you already know how.	Your sister has been on the phone for a long time. You want to ask her where the toys are she borrowed from you.	Your parents are deciding against buying the bike you want. You want to suggest a skateboard instead.
Take Responsibility for Self	Your teacher checks your work and excuses you to recess. You need to tell her that you aren't finished, but she is talking.	The neighbors are complimenting you on how well you mowed the lawn. Your brother actually did it.	Your older sister is explaining a new game to your brother. Your mom told you to call them to dinner.	Your parents are talking about raising your allowance. You need to tell them that *you*, not your brother, broke the T.V.
Stay Calm and Relaxed	Your teacher is talking to another student. You need to ask her about a hard math problem before you go home.	Your friends are about to leave for the pool. You want to ask your mom if you can go. She is talking to a friend.	You finished your chores, but your sisters haven't. They are talking. Mom said you can all go skating when chores are done.	Your mom is telling you what to buy at the store, and you need to tell her that you lost the money she gave you.
Solve Problems	Your classmate is holding the red marker and talking to a friend. You need to use it before the recess bell rings.	Your neighbors are in the yard talking about the flowers. You notice that the sprinkler is flooding their lawn.	Your brothers put some bread in the toaster and began talking about their baseball game. You think the toast might burn.	Dad comes home and begins telling you what a hard day he had. You need to tell him that you broke a window with your Frisbee.

54

Skill 6: Interrupting a Conversation
Activity

(This activity called Waiting for a Pause can also be used with Skill 7: Joining a Conversation. See the footnoted variations which would adapt it to other skills.*)

The materials needed are:

1. Chalkboard.
2. Chalk.

Draw two columns on the chalkboard. Head one, "Waited for a Pause," and the other one, "Did Not Wait for a Pause." List the children's names down the left side of the board.

A good time for this activity is during the snack. You may start the conversation by talking about some subject (a game, movie, or record) that the children will find very interesting or by encouraging a child to begin the conversation. The object of the game is to join the conversation as many times as possible by waiting for a pause.

The rules are:

1. Mark 1 point in the "Waited for a Pause" column each time a child joins in by waiting for a pause.
2. A child receives 1 point in the other column each time he/she *forgets* to wait for a pause when joining in.

3. At the end of the game, each person's total points will be determined by subtracting that person's points in the "Did Not Wait for a Pause" column from those in the "Waited for a Pause" column.
4. Everyone who has enough total points will earn a small prize *or* extra snack, extra play time, etc. (Decide in advance how many total points children need to score to earn a prize. The number of points should be high enough to challenge the children, but low enough to make it possible for most of them to earn a prize. The chalkboard should be in full view so that each child always knows how many points he/she has at the time.)

Give frequent Positive Feedback to children who join in by waiting for a pause. When children forget to wait for a pause, use an appropriate Teaching Strategy (e.g., the Teaching Interaction) to help them practice the skill.

---

*Variations may be made in this activity to use it with other skills and target behaviors by adding appropriate columns, such as: *saying, "Excuse me,"* for extra practice with Interrupting a Conversation; *ask about others* and *tell about yourself*, for Starting a Conversation and Keeping It Going; and *make a pause*, for let others talk.

Skill 6: Interrupting a Conversation
Home Note

Name _____ Instructors _____

During today's lesson we practiced interrupting a conversation the right way. We use this when other people are talking, and we need to ask or say something important.

Today's Objectives	Target Behaviors

Today's Objectives

To interrupt the right way, did the child:

	YES	NO
1. Use a pleasant face and voice?	____	____
2. Wait for a pause in the conversation?	____	____
3. Look directly at the person?	____	____
4. Say "Excuse me"?	____	____
5. Then talk?	____	____

Target Behaviors

		Score
A.	_____	____
B.	_____	____
C.	_____	____
D.	_____	____
E.	_____	____

Score, using this scale:
1 = Completely satisfied
2 = Satisfied
3 = Slightly satisfied
4 = Neither satisfied nor dissatisfied
5 = Slightly dissatisfied
6 = Dissatisfied
7 = Completely dissatisfied

The best thing your child did today in social skills was _____
_____

- -

Parents – Please Complete This Section and Return
Skill 6: Interrupting a Conversation

Name _____

The following objectives and target behaviors refer to those named above. Please mark or score your child in these areas and have him/her return this bottom section with your signature to the next social skills group.

Did your child meet the objectives of today's lesson at least once this week?

	YES	NO
Objective 1	____	____
Objective 2	____	____
Objective 3	____	____
Objective 4	____	____
Objective 5	____	____

Score your child on his/her target behaviors, using the 1-7 scale above:

Target Behavior A _____
Target Behavior B _____
Target Behavior C _____
Target Behavior D _____
Target Behavior E _____

Parent Signature _____ Date _____

Skill 6: Interrupting a Conversation
Homework

Name _____

1. Go up to two or more people who are talking and ask one of them a question, that is, interrupt their conversation the *right way*.

   a. What did you remember to wait for before you started talking? _____
   _____

   b. Then what did you say? _____
   _____

   c. What question did you ask? _____
   _____

   d. What did the other person do or say? _____

2. Repeat the exercise in Question 1 with some other people.

   a. What did you remember to wait for before you started talking? _____
   _____

   b. Then what did you say? _____
   _____

   c. What question did you ask? _____
   _____

   d. What did the other person do or say? _____

3. Give two reasons why it is good to interrupt a conversation the right way.

   a. _____
   _____

   b. _____
   _____

4. What are two things you could do if you interrupted the right way and still got in trouble for interrupting?

   a. _____
   _____

   b. _____
   _____

Session 7

Skill 7: Joining a Conversation

YOU MAY SUBSTITUTE naturally occurring events (lunch time, art projects, etc.) for items marked with an asterisk. Be sure to incidentally teach the day's skill, target behaviors, and the behaviors listed whether you use these activities or others. Remember that the dialogue provided in the session outlines (except for the lesson itself) is intended to be a model, not read or memorized verbatim. Read the dialogue over for main points and use your own spontaneous style. **Most of the dialogue and instructions are identical from skill to skill. For efficiency you may wish to attend only to the Relaxation Script number and the new information in the Skill Lesson.**

---

*Homework Completion and Free Play

In addition to today's skill and children's individual target behaviors, give special attention to taking responsibility, solving problems, and following directions (during Homework completion), and joining in, cooperating, problem solving, keeping a good attitude, and following directions (during free play).

Collect Homework and the bottom half of Home Notes; oversee free play and Homework completion or practice time.

Teacher 1:
(Scan papers to see which children have satisfactorily completed Homework; put aside Home Notes to check later.)

(children who completed it), you may go now and choose a game to play. (children who have not completed it), it's time for you to finish the Homework (or practice the skill) so that you can join the others.

(For children who habitually do not bring completed Homework, add more written questions or role play practice so that they finish about the same time as free play ends.)

Review Homework with children.

Teacher 1:
(Have children form a circle on the floor.)

Now let's look at the Homework you have done. I'm glad that (children who brought completed work) did their work at home. (a child who brought it), will you read your answer to Question _____?

(Have several children who brought their work read answers; ask for feedback from others. If you are using the Homework Progress Chart, allow children to color in the whole square or place a sticker in the square or color in part of it, depending on whether they brought completed Homework or finished it during free play.)

---

*Relaxation Training

In addition to today's skill and children's individual target behaviors, give special attention to keeping a calm body, solving problems, following directions, and keeping hands to self.

Lead relaxation training.

Teacher 1:
We are going to practice relaxing again. Relaxing will help you learn the new skill and help you face any problem.

(Have children find a place on the floor to lie down. Choose one child to turn off the lights.)

(Use Relaxation Script 3.)

● Introduce skill and list components.

Teacher 1:

Today we are going to talk about joining a conversation. To join a conversation, you:
- Use a pleasant face and voice.
- Look at the person.
- Wait for a pause.
- Say something on the topic.

· ·

● Role play appropriate example.

Teacher 1:

This is the right way to join a conversation. I'm with a friend, (Teacher 2). (Teacher 2) is talking to _____ about going roller-skating.

Teacher 2:

(talks with _____ while (Teacher 1) waits; there is a pause in the conversation)

Teacher 1:

(says something on the topic) Oh, yeah. I've been there before. It's really fun.

● Ask children for behavior components of skill.

Teacher 1:

How did you know that was the right way to join a conversation?
(children respond or are prompted)

● Role play inappropriate example.

Teacher 1:

This is the wrong way to join a conversation. I'm with a friend, (Teacher 2). (Teacher 2) is talking to _____ about going roller-skating.

Teacher 2:

(talks with _____)

Teacher 1:

(doesn't wait for a pause) Hey, you guys, want to see me make a basket from here? Watch this, you guys!

● Ask children for behavior components of skill.

Teacher 1:

What should have happened to make that the right way to join a conversation?
(children respond or are prompted)

· ·

● Ask children to role play.

Teacher 1:

Now it is your turn to role play. (Assign role play situa-tion.) I am going to call on someone who has been working really hard in the group by (specific on-task behaviors). _____ has been working really hard the whole time by (appropriate behaviors) and looks ready to be the first one to role play. _____, this is your role play.

(Describe the role play you have previously selected for this child from the role play sheet behind this session outline. Have each child role play the skill *correctly* at least one time.)

● Ask children to give Positive Feedback.

Teacher 1 or 2:

Good role playing. Who can give _____ *some Positive Feedback on his/her role play?*

(Call on child who is volunteering and paying attention.)

· ·

● Ask children for rationales for using skill.

Teacher 1:

Why do you think it is important to join a conversation the right way?
(children respond or are prompted)

Children:
- Helps people communicate better.
- People will want to listen to you more often.
- People will like you because you show interest in them.

· ·

● Lead children through reality check.

Teacher 1:

Sometimes you might try really hard to join a conversation, *and this might happen.* I'm with a friend, (Teacher 2). (Teacher 2) is talking to _____ about going roller-skating.

Teacher 2:

(talks with _____ while (Teacher 1) waits; there is a pause in the conversation)

Teacher 1:

(says something on the topic) Oh, yeah. I've been there before. It's really fun.

Teacher 2:

So what! Who really cares what you think anyway!

Teacher 1:

You just did everything right to join a conversation. *What should you do if this happens to you?*
(children respond or are prompted)

Children:
- Take a deep breath to get calm.
- Keep a good attitude.
- Walk away.
- Go find someone else to talk to.
- Try again later.

---

*Snack Time

In addition to today's skill and children's individual target behaviors, give special attention to following group rules, using conversation skills, cooperating, and solving problems.

Decide which children have earned all of snack.

Children may earn the entire snack or only a smaller portion if they join the snack in progress. Keep in mind how much difficulty a child has had following rules or practicing during the lesson and relaxation time to get an idea of how much time the child might need to practice to compensate for missed opportunities.

Dismiss children who have already earned snack time to the snack table.

Teacher 1:
OK, it's snack time now. (Teacher 2), who do you think has really been earning snack today?

Teacher 2:
Well, _____ has been really following the rules, having a still body, volunteering, and working on (his/her target behavior).

Teacher 1:
Yes, he/she really has. And I think _____ has also done a really good job of (specific behaviors). I'd like (child already named) to go to the snack table and pass out the napkins and (other child named) to go and pass out the cups.

(Continue dismissing children to the snack table by giving Positive Feedback for their accomplishments and assigning them a task at the snack table. If some children have not earned all of snack, have them practice as follows.)

Teacher 1:
_____, you need to sit here with me and practice (volunteering, keeping hands to self, etc.).

(Ask children questions from the lesson, have them role play, or do relaxation to give them opportunities to practice behaviors that were problematic during relaxation and/or the lesson. As the children practice, watch for a good attitude and effort in practicing and determine when each child seems to have made up for lost opportunities and achieved an acceptable level of competence in the skill or rule following.)

Ask children to clean up snack area.

Teacher 1:
OK, snack time is over now. We need to clean up. _____, would you get the garbage can and bring it around so everyone can throw away the garbage.

(Use Positive Feedback and other Teaching Strategies for cooperating and following directions during the cleanup.)

---

*Activity Time

In addition to today's skill and children's individual target behaviors, give special attention to following group rules, using conversation skills, cooperating, and solving problems.

Explain activity for today's lesson.

Teacher 1:
It's time for an activity now. Today we're going to (describe activity briefly). This is a time for us to practice our target behaviors and Joining a Conversation.

(Use Activity.)

Ask all the children to help clean up.

Teacher 1:
Now it's time for everyone to help clean up.

(Use Positive Feedback and other Teaching Strategies to help children work well together on cleanup. After cleanup, prompt children to return to circle.)

---

*Home Notes

In addition to today's skill and children's individual target behaviors, give special attention to following group rules and saying nice things.

Divide children into two groups and work on scoring Home Notes.

Teacher 1:
(a child), we are going to talk about how you did during today's session. Who can give (that child) some Positive Feedback and tell him/her good things about how he/she did on (target behavior)?

(Score the top half of the Home Note while the children are giving Positive Feedback. Ask for specific feedback for each of the child's target behaviors and add to it with comments you want to make, pointing out progress and areas needing improvement.)

(same child), now what do you think was the best thing you did in group today?
(child responds or is prompted)

Teacher 1:
That's good.

(Add specific descriptions of strong points.)

You might also try to (suggestions for improvement). Here is your Home Note.

(Repeat sequence with each child.)

---

*New Homework

In addition to today's skill and children's individual target behaviors, give special attention to following group rules and saying nice things.

Pass out Homework.

Teacher 1:
Here is your Homework. Be sure to do it and bring it back next time. Let's see what it says.

(Read aloud.)

If you need help, ask your parents or some other adult in your home.

Skill 7: Joining a Conversation
Role Plays

Situations Target Behaviors	School Problems (Teacher/Peers)	Neighborhood Problems	Sibling Problems	Parent Problems
Listen Carefully	Your teacher is talking to a student about a math problem. You have questions about that problem, too.	Your neighbor is going to pay your friend to do some yard work. You would like to help and can rake leaves really well.	Your two sisters are deciding which cartoons to watch on television. You would like to make a suggestion.	Your dad is telling your mom what yard work needs to be done. You would like to offer to mow the lawn.
Treat Others Nicely	A first-grader you know asks you to tell her friends about a trip you took to Disneyland last summer.	Two younger kids are trying to figure out how to use a skateboard. You know how to do lots of tricks on a skateboard.	Your sister is telling her friends how smart you are in math. You want to tell how she helps you a lot.	Your mom and grandma are talking about you. They want to hear about your hobbies. You are really in a hurry.
Join in with Others	Some kids in your class are talking about roller-skating. You are a good skater and won a race last week.	Some boys are trying to get a soccer game going. They need someone for a goalie. You'd like to try it.	Your brother is telling your friend how many home runs you hit in a game. You want to tell them about your next game.	Your parents are deciding where to go for vacation this summer. You would like to make some suggestions.
Keep a Good Attitude	Your teacher is telling your dad that you got a "B" on your spelling test. You really got an "A."	You hear two neighbors say that they think you walked on their flowers. You didn't do it.	Your brother is telling your dad that you didn't get your chores done. You have just finished them.	Your parents are deciding not to go out for pizza after all. You would like to suggest another place to go.
Take Responsibility for Self	Your teacher is telling the principal that you got all of your work done today. You actually have not finished your math.	Your neighbors are complimenting you for your nice garden. You know your brother did all of the work.	Your sister is telling your dad what a good job you did putting away her toys that you used. Your mom put them away.	You hear your mom tell your dad that she thinks you got all of your chores done today. You haven't really finished.
Stay Calm and Relaxed	Your classmates and teacher are about to decide not to go swimming today. You really want to go.	Your friend is telling his dad that your dog dug up their flowers. You know someone else's dog did it.	You are playing with your brother and sister. They are arguing about the rules of the game. You know this game well.	Your parents are about to decide to lower your weekly allowance. You want to offer to do more chores instead.
Solve Problems	Your friends are confused about the rules of a game. You know the rules of that game really well.	Your two friends are excited about a game and are talking really fast. You want to join but don't hear a pause.	Your brothers are arguing about which dessert to eat. You want to suggest eating half of each.	Your parents are talking about your weekend chores. They have forgotten that you want to stay over with a friend.

Skill 7: Joining a Conversation
Activity

(The activity provided for Skill 6: Interrupting a Conversation can also be used here with Skill 7.)

The materials needed are:

1. A chalkboard with the following listed on it: your favorite pet, what you like to do after school, a place you would like to visit, your favorite movie, and your favorite food.
2. A piece of paper and pencil for you to use in keeping score.

Have the children sit (eight at a time) in a circle or around a table. Have one of them begin a conversation by asking another child about one of the topics on the board. Each time a child joins the conversation by saying something on the topic without interrupting, he/she earns a point. Tell children they may add new topics only after they join in on the topic, i.e., they start with the topic being discussed and bring in a new topic by relating it to the original one. If a child joins the conversation on the topic and then adds a new topic, he/she would earn 2 points for the contribution. Tell the children it is to their advantage to keep their comments brief enough to allow others a turn since they will earn points each new time they join the conversation.

Skill 7: Joining a Conversation
Home Note

Name _____ Instructors _____

During today's lesson we practiced joining into an ongoing conversation with two or more other people.

Today's Objectives	Target Behaviors

Today's Objectives

To join a conversation, did the child:

	YES	NO
1. Use a pleasant face and voice?	____	____
2. Look at the person?	____	____
3. Wait for a pause?	____	____
4. Say something on the topic?	____	____

Target Behaviors

Score

A. _____ ____
B. _____ ____
C. _____ ____
D. _____ ____
E. _____ ____

Score, using this scale:
1 = Completely satisfied
2 = Satisfied
3 = Slightly satisfied
4 = Neither satisfied nor dissatisfied
5 = Slightly dissatisfied
6 = Dissatisfied
7 = Completely dissatisfied

The best thing your child did today in social skills was _____
_____

- -

Parents – Please Complete This Section and Return
Skill 7: Joining a Conversation

Name _____

The following objectives and target behaviors refer to those named above. Please mark or score your child in these areas and have him/her return this bottom section with your signature to the next social skills group.

Did your child meet the objectives of today's lesson at least once this week?

	YES	NO
Objective 1	____	____
Objective 2	____	____
Objective 3	____	____
Objective 4	____	____

Score your child on his/her target behaviors, using the 1-7 scale above:

Target Behavior A _____
Target Behavior B _____
Target Behavior C _____
Target Behavior D _____
Target Behavior E _____

Parent Signature _____ Date _____

SCHOOL OF EDUCATION
CURRICULUM LABORATORY
UM-DEARBORN

Skill 7: Joining a Conversation
Homework

Name _____

1. Go up to two or more people who are talking and join in their conversation. What are three things you remembered to do before you started talking?

    a. _____
    _____

    b. _____
    _____

    c. _____
    _____

2. Describe the conversation.

    a. What was the conversation about? _____
    _____

    b. What did you say? _____
    _____

3. Give two reasons why it is important to join a conversation the right way.

    a. _____
    _____

    b. _____
    _____

4. Name two things you could do if you tried to join a conversation the right way, but you were ignored.

    a. _____
    _____

    b. _____
    _____

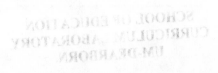

Session 8

Skill 8: Starting a Conversation and Keeping it Going

YOU MAY SUBSTITUTE naturally occurring events (lunch time, art projects, etc.) for items marked with an asterisk. Be sure to incidentally teach the day's skill, target behaviors, and the behaviors listed whether you use these activities or others. Remember that the dialogue provided in the session outlines (except for the lesson itself) is intended to be a model, not read or memorized verbatim. Read the dialogue over for main points and use your own spontaneous style. **Most of the dialogue and instructions are identical from skill to skill. For efficiency you may wish to attend only to the Relaxation Script number and the new information in the Skill Lesson.**

*Homework Completion and Free Play

In addition to today's skill and children's individual target behaviors, give special attention to taking responsibility, solving problems, and following directions (during Homework completion), and joining in, cooperating, problem solving, keeping a good attitude, and following directions (during free play).

Collect Homework and the bottom half of Home Notes; oversee free play and Homework completion or practice time.

Teacher 1:
(Scan papers to see which children have satisfactorily completed Homework; put aside Home Notes to check later.)

(children who completed it), you may go now and choose a game to play. (children who have not completed it), it's time for you to finish the Homework (or practice the skill) so that you can join the others.

(For children who habitually do not bring completed Homework, add more written questions or role play practice so that they finish about the same time as free play ends.)

Review Homework with children.

Teacher 1:
(Have children form a circle on the floor.)

Now let's look at the Homework you have done. I'm glad that (children who brought completed work) did their work at home. (a child who brought it), will you read your answer to Question _____?

(Have several children who brought their work read answers; ask for feedback from others. If you are using the Homework Progress Chart, allow children to color in the whole square or place a sticker in the square or color in part of it, depending on whether they brought completed Homework or finished it during free play.)

*Relaxation Training

In addition to today's skill and children's individual target behaviors, give special attention to keeping a calm body, solving problems, following directions, and keeping hands to self.

Lead relaxation training.

Teacher 1:
We are going to practice relaxing again. Relaxing will help you learn the new skill and help you face any problem.

(Have children find a place on the floor to lie down. Choose one child to turn off the lights.)

(Use Relaxation Script 3.)

Skill Lesson 8

● **Introduce skill and list components.**

Teacher 1:
Today we are going to talk about starting a conversation and keeping it going. To start a conversation and keep it going, you:
▪ Use a pleasant face and voice.
▪ Look at the person.
▪ Ask questions about the other person.
▪ Tell about yourself.

. . . .

● **Role play appropriate example.**

Teacher 1:
This is the right way to start a conversation and keep it going. I'm on the playground, and I'm going to start a conversation with a new kid.
Hi, I'm Joyce. You're new here, aren't you? What's your name?

Teacher 2:
I'm Allan. Yeah, today is my first day at this school. I'm in the fourth grade. What grade are you in?

Teacher 1:
I'm in the third grade, but I think we ride the same bus, bus 40.

Teacher 2:
That *is* my bus. We must live in the same neighborhood. What is your address?

Teacher 1:
200 Center Street. What's your address?

Teacher 2:
210 Center Street.

Teacher 1:
We do live close to each other. Maybe you can ask your mom if you can come over to my house today after school.

Teacher 2:
That would be fun.

● **Ask children for behavior components of skill.**

Teacher 1:
How did you know that was the right way to start a conversation and keep it going?
(children respond or are prompted)

● **Role play inappropriate example.**

Teacher 1:
This is the wrong way to start a conversation and keep it going. I'm on the playground, and I'm going to start a

conversation with a new kid.
Hi, I'm Joyce. You're new here, aren't you? What's your name?

Teacher 2:
Allan.

Teacher 1:
I'm in third grade. What grade are you in?

Teacher 2:
Fourth.

Teacher 1:
I think I saw you on my bus this morning.

Teacher 2:
I don't know. (shrugs; looks away)

● **Ask children for behavior components of skill.**

Teacher 1:
What should have happened to make that the right way to start a conversation and keep it going?
(children respond or are prompted)

. . . .

● **Ask children to role play.**

Teacher 1:
Now it is your turn to role play. (Assign role play situation.) I am going to call on someone who has been working really hard in the group by (specific on-task behaviors). _____ has been working really hard the whole time by (appropriate behaviors) and looks ready to be the first one to role play. _____, this is your role play.

(Describe the role play you have previously selected for this child from the role play sheet behind this session outline. Have each child role play the skill *correctly* at least one time.)

● **Ask children to give Positive Feedback.**

Teacher 1 or 2:
Good role playing. Who can give _____ *some Positive Feedback on his/her role play?*

(Call on child who is volunteering and paying attention.)

. . . .

● **Ask children for rationales for using skill.**

Teacher 1:
Why do you think it is important to start a conversation and keep it going?
(children respond or are prompted)

68

Children:
- You will seem friendlier.
- You can make more friends.
- You can get to know others better, and they can get to know you.
- You make others feel important when you ask about them.

. . . .

● **Lead children through reality check.**

Teacher 1:
Sometimes you might try really hard to start a conversation and keep it going, *and this might happen.* I'm on the playground, and I'm going to start a conversation with a new kid.
Hi, I'm Joyce. You're new here, aren't you? What's your name?

Teacher 2:
Allan.

Teacher 1:
I'm in the third grade. What grade are you in?

Teacher 2:
I'm in the fourth grade, and I don't talk to third-graders!

Teacher 1:
You just did everything right to start a conversation and keep it going. *What should you do if this happens to you?* (children respond or are prompted)

Children:
- Take a deep breath to get calm.
- Keep a good attitude.
- Walk away.
- Go find someone else to talk to.
- Try again later.

---

*Snack Time

In addition to today's skill and children's individual target behaviors, give special attention to following group rules, using conversation skills, cooperating, and solving problems.

Decide which children have earned all of snack.

Children may earn the entire snack or only a smaller portion if they join the snack in progress. Keep in mind how much difficulty a child has had following rules or practicing during the lesson and relaxation time to get an idea of how much time the child might need to practice to compensate for missed opportunities.

Dismiss children who have already earned snack time to the snack table.

Teacher 1:
OK, it's snack time now. (Teacher 2), who do you think has really been earning snack today?

Teacher 2:
Well, _____ has been really following the rules, having a still body, volunteering, and working on (his/her target behavior).

Teacher 1:
Yes, he/she really has. And I think _____ has also done a really good job of (specific behaviors). I'd like (child already named) to go to the snack table and pass out the napkins and (other child named) to go and pass out the cups.

(Continue dismissing children to the snack table by giving Positive Feedback for their accomplishments and assigning them a task at the snack table. If some children have not earned all of snack, have them practice as follows.)

Teacher 1:
_____, you need to sit here with me and practice (volunteering, keeping hands to self, etc.).

(Ask children questions from the lesson, have them role play, or do relaxation to give them opportunities to practice behaviors that were problematic during relaxation and/or the lesson. As the children practice, watch for a good attitude and effort in practicing and determine when each child seems to have made up for lost opportunities and achieved an acceptable level of competence in the skill or rule following.)

Ask children to clean up snack area.

Teacher 1:
OK, snack time is over now. We need to clean up. _____, would you get the garbage can and bring it around so everyone can throw away the garbage.

(Use Positive Feedback and other Teaching Strategies for cooperating and following directions during the cleanup.)

---

*Activity Time

In addition to today's skill and children's individual target behaviors, give special attention to following group rules, using conversation skills, cooperating, and solving problems.

Explain activity for today's lesson.

Teacher 1:
It's time for an activity now. Today we're going to (describe activity briefly). This is a time for us to practice our target behaviors and Starting a Conversation and Keeping it Going.

(Use Activity.)

Ask all the children to help clean up.

Teacher 1:
Now it's time for everyone to help clean up.

(Use Positive Feedback and other Teaching Strategies to help children work well together on cleanup. After cleanup, prompt children to return to circle.)

---

*Home Notes

In addition to today's skill and children's individual target behaviors, give special attention to following group rules and saying nice things.

Divide children into two groups and work on scoring Home Notes.

Teacher 1:
(a child), we are going to talk about how you did during today's session. Who can give (that child) some Positive Feedback and tell him/her good things about how he/she did on (target behavior)?

(Score the top half of the Home Note while the children are giving Positive Feedback. Ask for specific feedback for each of the child's target behaviors and add to it with comments you want to make, pointing out progress and areas needing improvement.)

(same child), now what do you think was the best thing you did in group today?
(child responds or is prompted)

Teacher 1:
That's good.

(Add specific descriptions of strong points.)

You might also try to (suggestions for improvement). Here is your Home Note.

(Repeat sequence with each child.)

---

*New Homework

In addition to today's skill and children's individual target behaviors, give special attention to following group rules and saying nice things.

Pass out Homework.

Teacher 1:

Here is your Homework. Be sure to do it and bring it back next time. Let's see what it says.

(Read aloud.)

If you need help, ask your parents or some other adult in your home.

Skill 8: Starting a Conversation and Keeping it Going
Role Plays

Situations / Target Behaviors	School Problems (Teacher/Peers)	Neighborhood Problems	Sibling Problems	Parent Problems
Listen Carefully	Your teacher is talking about a fishing trip he took. You want to find out more about it.	Your friend has been on a long vacation. He just got home. You want to find out what he did.	Your brother just got back from summer camp. You want to hear all about it.	Your mom saw a movie that you have been curious about. You want to find out about it.
Treat Others Nicely	You see a kid sitting all alone at recess time. You want to talk to him.	Your neighbor's brothers left town for a week. You see him by himself in his front yard.	Your sister is sad because her basketball team lost a game. You see her by herself at recess.	Your mom has been cleaning house by herself all day. You just got home from school.
Join in with Others	You see a kid you like on the playground. You have not seen her for a few days, and you want to find out what she's doing.	A new kid moved in next door to you last week. You see her outside in her yard and want to talk to her.	You're at the dinner table with your sister. You want to find out about her softball game.	You just got home from school. Your dad is reading the paper, and you want to tell him about your game today.
Keep a Good Attitude	Your teacher paired everyone in your classroom with a partner for art. You're the only boy with a girl partner.	You wanted to go swimming today, but your dad is making you do yard work. You see your neighbor out mowing his lawn.	Your brother's chore is to sweep the garage. Today your mom makes you go out and help him. It will take you an hour.	You wanted to sleep in this morning but your mom wants you to go grocery shopping with her. You are in the car with her.
Take Responsibility for Self	There's a new kid in your classroom. You are sitting next to her during art time.	A new family moved to your neighborhood. Today you see two of their kids playing out on the sidewalk.	You are cleaning up your brother's toys that you used. He comes in to help you.	A friend of your dad's came over to visit him. Your dad got a phone call, and you are alone with his friend in the yard.
Stay Calm and Relaxed	An older boy whom you've never seen before sits next to you on the school bus.	You are standing in a long line at the movies. An older boy is in front of you. You feel like talking to someone.	Your brother and sister were arguing at the dinner table. Now they are quiet, and you want to tell about your game.	Your mom wants you to babysit her friend's little girl so that they can go shopping. You take her out in the yard.
Solve Problems	You're waiting for your dad to come and pick you up after school. He's really late. You see a kid playing near by.	You are taking care of a neighbor's yard while she is out of town. A friend you've not seen lately comes walking by.	You wanted to go skating with your friends, but you have to babysit your little sister all night. The T.V. is broken.	You and a friend are waiting for his mom to pick you up. It's taking longer than you had expected.

Skill 8: Starting a Conversation and Keeping it Going
Activity

(The activity provided for Skill 6: Interrupting a Conversation notes variations that may also be used here.)

The materials needed are:

1. A chalkboard and chalk.
2. A set of cards, each naming a television, cartoon, or movie character with whom the children are familiar (there should be as many cards as there are children playing the game).
3. Small prizes (stickers, prizes from caramel corn boxes, etc.).
4. A pencil and piece of paper for each child.

To begin, have each child pick one card, without showing it to anyone or telling anyone the name on the card. Tell the children to pretend to be the characters named on their cards. The object of the activity is to determine the identities of as many of the other children as possible in a set time (10-15 minutes). This is done by approaching other children, pairing off with them, and *asking* and *answering* questions about their characters (e.g., "What movie/television series/cartoon strip do you live in?" "Do you wear a red and blue suit?" etc.) (The children don't need to remain in the circle during this time.)

The rules are:

1. A child can't guess the other person's "name" until he/she has asked at least three other questions about the character. If the child guesses the other person's name before doing this, the person asked doesn't have to give his/her "name."
2. A child must answer all *appropriate* questions (see Rule 1) and must answer them honestly.
3. After a child has determined the other person's "name" (if he/she has answered all the questions), the first child may find someone else with whom to talk.
4. The children can write down "names" that they have figured out, to help them remember.
5. At the end of the allotted time, everyone returns to the circle. Each person in turn will introduce to the group everyone whose "name" he/she has discovered.
6. A child gets one prize for every person whose "name" he/she has discovered.

Watch and give Positive Feedback for keeping a conversation going. To help the children ask appropriate questions, write on the chalkboard a number of examples and bring them to the attention of the children. Those children who have particular difficulty asking appropriate questions can be coached. Also, children who have difficulty remembering to wait for a pause can be helped to practice this skill.

Skill 8: Starting a Conversation and Keeping it Going
Home Note

Name _____ Instructors _____

During today's lesson we practiced starting conversations with other people and taking the initiative in keeping them going. This helps others to get to know us better, and we can get to know other people better.

Today's Objectives			Target Behaviors	
To start a conversation and keep it going, did the child:				Score
	YES	NO	A. _____	_____
1. Use a pleasant face and voice?	_____	_____	B. _____	_____
2. Look at the person?	_____	_____	C. _____	_____
3. Ask questions about the other person?	_____	_____	D. _____	_____
4. Tell about himself/herself?	_____	_____	E. _____	_____

Score, using this scale:
1 = Completely satisfied
2 = Satisfied
3 = Slightly satisfied
4 = Neither satisfied nor dissatisfied
5 = Slightly dissatisfied
6 = Dissatisfied
7 = Completely dissatisfied

The best thing your child did today in social skills was _____
_____

- -

Parents – Please Complete This Section and Return
Skill 8: Starting a Conversation and Keeping It Going

Name _____

The following objectives and target behaviors refer to those named above. Please mark or score your child in these areas and have him/her return this bottom section with your signature to the next social skills group.

Did your child meet the objectives of today's lesson at least once this week?			Score your child on his/her target behaviors, using the 1-7 scale above:
	YES	NO	
Objective 1	_____	_____	Target Behavior A _____
Objective 2	_____	_____	Target Behavior B _____
Objective 3	_____	_____	Target Behavior C _____
Objective 4	_____	_____	Target Behavior D _____
			Target Behavior E _____

Parent Signature _____ Date _____

74

Skill 8: Starting a Conversation and Keeping It Going
Homework

Name _____

1. What are three important things to remember when starting a conversation and keeping it going?

   a. _____
   _____

   b. _____
   _____

   c. _____
   _____

2. Start a conversation with someone.

   a. Who were you talking with? _____
   _____

   b. How did you start the conversation? _____
   _____

   c. What did you ask about the other person? _____
   _____

   d. What did you tell him or her about yourself?_____
   _____

3. Give three reasons why it is important to know how to start a conversation and keep it going.

   a. _____
   _____

   b. _____
   _____

   c. _____
   _____

Session 9

Skill 9: Sharing

YOU MAY SUBSTITUTE naturally occurring events (lunch time, art projects, etc.) for items marked with an asterisk. Be sure to incidentally teach the day's skill, target behaviors, and the behaviors listed whether you use these activities or others. Remember that the dialogue provided in the session outlines (except for the lesson itself) is intended to be a model, not read or memorized verbatim. Read the dialogue over for main points and use your own spontaneous style. **Most of the dialogue and instructions are identical from skill to skill. For efficiency you may wish to attend only to the Relaxation Script number and the new information in the Skill Lesson.**

*Homework Completion and Free Play

In addition to today's skill and children's individual target behaviors, give special attention to taking responsibility, solving problems, and following directions (during Homework completion), and joining in, cooperating, problem solving, keeping a good attitude, and following directions (during free play).

Collect Homework and the bottom half of Home Notes; oversee free play and Homework completion or practice time.

Teacher 1:
(Scan papers to see which children have satisfactorily completed Homework; put aside Home Notes to check later.)

(children who completed it), you may go now and choose a game to play. (children who have not completed it), it's time for you to finish the Homework (or practice the skill) so that you can join the others.

(For children who habitually do not bring completed Homework, add more written questions or role play practice so that they finish about the same time as free play ends.)

Review Homework with children.

Teacher 1:
(Have children form a circle on the floor.)

Now let's look at the Homework you have done. I'm glad that (children who brought completed work) did their work at home. (a child who brought it), will you read your answer to Question _____?

(Have several children who brought their work read answers; ask for feedback from others. If you are using the Homework Progress Chart, allow children to color in the whole square or place a sticker in the square or color in part of it, depending on whether they brought completed Homework or finished it during free play.)

*Relaxation Training

In addition to today's skill and children's individual target behaviors, give special attention to keeping a calm body, solving problems, following directions, and keeping hands to self.

Lead relaxation training.

Teacher 1:
We are going to practice relaxing again. Relaxing will help you learn the new skill and help you face any problem.

(Have children find a place on the floor to lie down. Choose one child to turn off the lights.)

(Use Relaxation Script 4.)

Skill Lesson 9

● Introduce skill and list components.

Teacher 1:
Today we are going to talk about sharing. To share, you:
- Use a pleasant face and voice.
- Divide up something that there's not much of, so others can also have some (if appropriate).
- Take turns (if appropriate).

. . . .

● Role play appropriate example.

Teacher 1:
This is the right way to share. I'm getting a snack. There's only one cookie left, and my sister comes in.

Teacher 2:
Hi, what are you doing?

Teacher 1:
I'm eating the last cookie. Do you want half of it? (offers to share cookie)

● Ask children for behavior components of skill.

Teacher 1:
How did you know that was the right way to share?
(children respond or are prompted)

● Role play inappropriate example.

Teacher 1:
This is the wrong way to share. I'm getting a snack. There's only one cookie left, and my sister comes in.

Teacher 2:
Hi, what are you doing?

Teacher 1:
I'm eating this cookie. It's the last one.

● Ask children for behavior components of skill.

Teacher 1:
What should have happened to make that the right way to share?
(children respond or are prompted)

. . . .

● Ask children to role play.

Teacher 1:
Now it is your turn to role play. (Assign role play situation.) I am going to call on someone who has been working really hard in the group by (specific on-task behaviors). _____ has been working really hard the

whole time by (appropriate behaviors) and looks ready to be the first one to role play. _____, this is your role play.

(Describe the role play you have previously selected for this child from the role play sheet behind this session outline. Have each child role play the skill *correctly* at least one time.)

● Ask children to give Positive Feedback.

Teacher 1 or 2:
Good role playing. Who can give _____ *some Positive Feedback on his/her role play?*

(Call on child who is volunteering and paying attention.)

. . . .

● Ask children for rationales for using skill.

Teacher 1:
Why do you think it is important to share?
(children respond or are prompted)

Children:
- So others will want to share with you.
- To make more friends.
- To make others feel good.

. . . .

● Lead children through reality check.

Teacher 1:
Sometimes you might try really hard to share, *and this might happen.* I'm getting a snack. There's only one cookie left, and my sister comes in.

Teacher 2:
Hi, what are you doing?

Teacher 1:
I'm eating the last cookie. Do you want half of it? (offers to share cookie)

Teacher 2:
I want the whole thing! (grabs cookie)

Teacher 1:
You just did everything right to share. *What should you do if this happens to you?*
(children respond or are prompted)

Children:
- Take a deep breath to get calm.
- Keep a good attitude.
- Ask her nicely to share with you.
- Ignore her and find something else to do.

*Snack Time

In addition to today's skill and children's individual target behaviors, give special attention to following group rules, using conversation skills, cooperating, and solving problems.

Decide which children have earned all of snack.

Children may earn the entire snack or only a smaller portion if they join the snack in progress. Keep in mind how much difficulty a child has had following rules or practicing during the lesson and relaxation time to get an idea of how much time the child might need to practice to compensate for missed opportunities.

Dismiss children who have already earned snack time to the snack table.

Teacher 1:
OK, it's snack time now. (Teacher 2), who do you think has really been earning snack today?

Teacher 2:
Well, _____ has been really following the rules, having a still body, volunteering, and working on (his/her target behavior).

Teacher 1:
Yes, he/she really has. And I think _____ has also done a really good job of (specific behaviors). I'd like (child already named) to go to the snack table and pass out the napkins and (other child named) to go and pass out the cups.

(Continue dismissing children to the snack table by giving Positive Feedback for their accomplishments and assigning them a task at the snack table. If some children have not earned all of snack, have them practice as follows.)

Teacher 1:
_____, you need to sit here with me and practice (volunteering, keeping hands to self, etc.).

(Ask children questions from the lesson, have them role play, or do relaxation to give them opportunities to practice behaviors that were problematic during relaxation and/or the lesson. As the children practice, watch for a good attitude and effort in practicing and determine when each child seems to have made up for lost opportunities and achieved an acceptable level of competence in the skill or rule following.)

Ask children to clean up snack area.

Teacher 1:
OK, snack time is over now. We need to clean up. _____, would you get the garbage can and bring it around so everyone can throw away the garbage.

(Use Positive Feedback and other Teaching Strategies for cooperating and following directions during the cleanup.)

---

*Activity Time

In addition to today's skill and children's individual target behaviors, give special attention to following group rules, using conversation skills, cooperating, and solving problems.

Explain activity for today's lesson.

Teacher 1:
It's time for an activity now. Today we're going to (describe activity briefly). This is a time for us to practice our target behaviors and Sharing.

(Use Activity.)

Ask all the children to help clean up.

Teacher 1:
Now it's time for everyone to help clean up.

(Use Positive Feedback and other Teaching Strategies to help children work well together on cleanup. After cleanup, prompt children to return to circle.)

---

*Home Notes

In addition to today's skill and children's individual target behaviors, give special attention to following group rules and saying nice things.

Divide children into two groups and work on scoring Home Notes.

Teacher 1:

(a child), we are going to talk about how you did during today's session. Who can give (that child) some Positive Feedback and tell him/her good things about how he/she did on (target behavior)?

(Score the top half of the Home Note while the children are giving Positive Feedback. Ask for specific feedback for each of the child's target behaviors and add to it with comments you want to make, pointing out progress and areas needing improvement.)

(same child), now what do you think was the best thing you did in group today?
(child responds or is prompted)

Teacher 1:
That's good.

(Add specific descriptions of strong points.)

You might also try to (suggestions for improvement). Here is your Home Note.

(Repeat sequence with each child.)

---

*New Homework

In addition to today's skill and children's individual target behaviors, give special attention to following group rules and saying nice things.

Pass out Homework.

Teacher 1:
Here is your Homework. Be sure to do it and bring it back next time. Let's see what it says.

(Read aloud.)

If you need help, ask your parents or some other adult in your home.

Relaxation Script 4

(This script may be used in conjunction with Skills 9, 10, and 11. Please review the section on relaxation training in Chapter 5 of the Guide.)

Today we're going to practice how to relax our bodies and keep calm by taking slow, deep breaths.

As I count to three, breathe in slowly, and as you breathe out, think to yourself "I AM CALM." (count aloud slowly) One . . . two . . . three. (pause) Relax. Notice how your body feels more relaxed and how calm you feel. (pause) As you take a slow, deep breath and let it go, you are letting out tensions and worries.

Now think about your face. If your forehead, mouth, or eyes feel tense, relax them, and let your face go smooth. (pause) As I count to three, breathe in slowly, and as you breathe out, think the words "I AM CALM." (count aloud slowly) One . . . two . . . three. (pause) Relax.

Now think about your shoulders. If they feel tight, let them go soft and loose. (pause) As I count to three, breathe in slowly, and as you breathe out, think the words "I AM CALM." (count aloud slowly) One . . . two . . . three. (pause) Relax.

Now think about your arms and hands. If they feel tight, relax them, and let them flop loosely and quietly at your sides. As I count to three, breathe in slowly, and as you breathe out, think the words "I AM CALM." (count aloud slowly) One . . . two . . . three. (pause) Relax.

Think about your stomach. If it feels tight, let it go soft. (pause) As I count to three, breathe in slowly, and as you breathe out, think the words "I AM CALM." (count aloud slowly) One . . . two . . . three. (pause) Relax.

Now think about your legs and feet. If they feel tight, relax them and let them flop softly and quietly on the floor. (pause) As I count to three, breathe in slowly, and as you breathe out, think the words "I AM CALM." (count aloud slowly) One . . . two . . . three. (pause) Relax.

Now that you are relaxed, let's talk about feelings and how they can make your body feel. When you are upset or angry, your body feels tense. When you are tense, it is difficult to solve problems. But when you are relaxed and calm, problem solving is easier, and you can feel better about yourself.

Let's imagine a situation at home. You're watching your favorite T.V. program and your mom asks you to turn it off so she can listen to the radio. Your body begins to feel tense; you begin to feel angry. Think of the tense muscles, maybe in your face, arms, and stomach. (pause) Now relax them. (pause) As I count to three, breathe in slowly, and as you breathe out, think the words "I AM CALM." (count aloud slowly) One . . . two . . . three. (pause) Relax. Now that you are relaxed, you feel better. You can keep calm by breathing deeply and relaxing your body. (pause) One more time, keep your body calm and relaxed and think of the time when someone wanted something at the same time you wanted something else. (pause) As I count to three, breathe in slowly, and as you breathe out, think the words "I AM CALM." (count aloud slowly) One . . . two . . . three. (pause) Relax. Now that you are relaxed, you feel better. You can keep calm by breathing deeply and relaxing your body. (pause) One more time, keep your body calm and relaxed and think of the time when someone wanted something at the same time you wanted something else. (pause) As I count to three, breathe in slowly, and as you breathe out, think the words "I AM CALM." (count aloud slowly) One . . . two . . . three. (pause) Relax. Now that you are calm and relaxed, you can solve your problems without getting upset.

Now think of another time at home or at school when you were upset or angry. (pause and give children a chance to think of their own situations) Imagine yourself in this situation. Think about how your body feels; your arms, stomach, and face may feel tense. (pause) If they are feeling tight, let them go. (pause) As I count to three, breathe in slowly, and as you breathe out, think the words "I AM CALM." (count aloud slowly) One . . . two . . . three. (pause) Relax.

Now your body feels calm and relaxed. You feel good. The next time you begin to feel upset or angry, remember how you feel right now. You can make your body feel calm all the time. When you want to relax, think about your body, breathe in slowly, and let go of all the tension.

Skill 9: Sharing
Role Plays

Situations / Target Behaviors	School Problems (Teacher/Peers)	Neighborhood Problems	Sibling Problems	Parent Problems
Listen Carefully	Your team captain tells you and your teammate to practice hitting the ball. There is only one bat.	Your neighbor explains to you how to water her lawn. Your friend wants to help you with the hose.	Your big brother is telling you about his game and how thirsty he is. You are drinking a soda.	Dad is bringing you a toy if you get along with the babysitter. You both want to ride bikes, but there's only one.
Treat Others Nicely	Your desk is near the new kid's. You notice during art activity time that he doesn't have any crayons.	You just got a new yo-yo. A little neighbor kid comes by and asks you what you're doing.	You just picked up the last piece of pizza. Your brother asks you nicely if he can have half of it.	You took some money to the store to buy comic books. Your mom doesn't have enough money for the groceries and wants you to help pay.
Join in with Others	You are on the swing at recess time. Some kids come over and stand near the swing. You think they may want a turn.	You hear two neighbor kids complaining that they have nothing to do. You just got a new soccer ball for your birthday.	Your little sister and you are skateboarding. Your older sister would like to play, too, but there are only two skateboards.	Your parents are counting some change they have been saving for your roller skates. You have some change saved, too.
Keep a Good Attitude	You are on a school picnic. The boy next to you is looking at the cupcake you brought in your lunch.	A neighbor gave you a toy for helping him. His little daughter asks you what you are playing with.	You are drinking a soda. Your babysitter suggests that you share it with your brother.	Your dad tells you to share some birthday toys your grandma gave you with your little brother.
Take Responsibility for Self	You get to clean chalkboard erasers this week. A girl who has never done it asks if she can have a turn.	You take the kids you are babysitting with you to the 7-11. You buy some gum. They don't have any money.	You are taking your little brother to the show. He lost his money along the way. You have some extra money.	Your mom bought you a comic book that you are reading. The friend you invited over has just arrived.
Stay Calm and Relaxed	You are getting a drink at the fountain at recess time. A small kid comes up and asks for a turn.	You are sharing some candy with a neighbor. Two more kids walk up and watch you.	You bought ice cream cones for your sister and yourself. She drops hers on the ground and begins to cry.	A neighbor paid you for all of the hard work you did for him. Your dad tells you to share the money with your sister.
Solve Problems	You want to show your teacher some tricks on the monkey bars. Others are waiting in line to use the bars.	You have two pieces of candy. You give one to a friend, and after she unwraps it, she drops it in the dirt.	It's a hot day, and you just got the last Popsicle out of the freezer. Your sister walks in.	You are standing on the diving board trying to get your mom's attention when a kid gets in line to use the board.

Skill 9: Sharing
Activity

(This activity called Marble Game can also be used with Skill 2: Following Directions, Skill 3: Giving and Receiving Positive Feedback, Skill 12: Asking for Clear Directions, Skill 14: Using Positive Consequences, and in general for practicing a good attitude. The activities provided for Skill 10: Offering to Help and for Skill 11: Compromising can also be used here with Skill 9.)

The materials needed are:

1. Enough marbles so that each child may have one.
2. Chalk.
3. Candy treats and small prizes.
4. A rules board.
5. Three Styrofoam cups or markers—one with "Give" written on one side, one with "Get" written on one side, and one with three prizes in it marked "Share with a friend."

The object of the game is to win prizes by hitting them with marbles rolled across the floor.

The rules are:

1. Move any furniture out of the way.
2. Draw a chalk line on the floor that is 10 feet long, 15 feet away from and parallel to a wall.
3. Each person may have one marble shooter.
4. Everyone will stay kneeling behind the chalk line and will take turns shooting marbles at the prizes that have been scattered on the floor near the wall. All prizes hit may be kept.
5. A child must not shoot until the person who shot before her/him has retrieved her/his marble and is again *behind* the chalk line.
6. If a child shoots out of turn or before everyone is behind the line, she/he loses the next turn!
7. If the child's marble hits the marker that says "Give," she/he must give away any one of her/his prizes to another child of her/his choice. If the child's marble

hits the marker saying "Get," that child may pick any prize she/he chooses from any of the other children.
8. You are the referee and will judge which prizes a marble has hit. If you are not ready when a child shoots, she/he misses that turn.
9. Children must save their prizes, not eat them.

Hold the rules board so that it can be seen by all of the children. Have the children take turns reading the rules, then assign children to move furniture, draw the chalk line, etc. If they fail to ask for clear directions (e.g., "Where should I move the chairs?" "Where should I draw the chalk line?" etc.), ask "Do you understand?" If necessary, use more specific prompts (e.g., "Do you know where the chairs should go?").

While the children are readying the room, scatter the prizes on the floor near the wall. Place the markers saying "Give," "Get," and "Share with a friend" among the prizes so that the words are not visible to the children.

Play the game for 10 to 15 minutes. Give Positive Feedback for spontaneous usage of skills being practiced (e.g., follow directions; ask, not tell; give and receive Positive Feedback; use positive consequences; good attitude; and take responsibility *just* for self).

If you are working with a partner you can use the appropriate Teaching Strategies to help a child practice the skills by first removing him from the game. If you are working alone, you will have to stop the game, have the child practice the appropriate behavior, and then let the game resume. At the end of the game those children who worked hard to practice the skills and their target behaviors (e.g., keeping a good attitude when someone else got to take away a favorite prize, keeping a good attitude even though not hitting any prizes) can be named and allowed to choose one of the remaining unclaimed prizes in return for working hard.

Skill 9: Sharing
Home Note

Name _____ Instructors _____

During today's lesson we practiced sharing what we have with others when there's not enough to go around and also sharing by taking turns with others.

Today's Objectives	**Target Behaviors**

Today's Objectives

To share, did the child:

	YES	NO
1. Use a pleasant face and voice?	_____	_____
2. Divide up something there's not much of so others can also have some?	_____	_____
3. Take turns?	_____	_____

Target Behaviors

                                               Score

A. _____ _____
B. _____ _____
C. _____ _____
D. _____ _____
E. _____ _____

Score, using this scale:
1 = Completely satisfied
2 = Satisfied
3 = Slightly satisfied
4 = Neither satisfied nor dissatisfied
5 = Slightly dissatisfied
6 = Dissatisfied
7 = Completely dissatisfied

The best thing your child did today in social skills was _____

_____

- -

Parents – Please Complete This Section and Return
Skill 9: Sharing

Name _____

The following objectives and target behaviors refer to those named above. Please mark or score your child in these areas and have him/her return this bottom section with your signature to the next social skills group.

Did your child meet the objectives of today's lesson at least once this week?

	YES	NO
Objective 1	_____	_____
Objective 2	_____	_____
Objective 3	_____	_____

Score your child on his/her target behaviors, using the 1-7 scale above:

Target Behavior A _____

Target Behavior B _____

Target Behavior C _____

Target Behavior D _____

Target Behavior E _____

Parent Signature _____ Date _____

Skill 9: Sharing
Homework

Name _____

1. Write down two times you shared at home, school, or elsewhere this week.

   Time 1:
   a. Who did you share with? _____

   _____

   b. How did you share? _____

   _____

   _____

   _____

   Time 2:
   a. Who did you share with? _____

   _____

   b. How did you share? _____

   _____

   _____

   _____

2. Give three reasons why it is good to share with others.

   a. _____

   _____

   b. _____

   _____

   c. _____

   _____

3. Tell about a time someone shared with you and how it made you feel.

   a. How did the other person share? _____

   _____

   b. How did you feel? _____

   _____

Session 10

Skill 10: Offering to Help

YOU MAY SUBSTITUTE naturally occurring events (lunch time, art projects, etc.) for items marked with an asterisk. Be sure to incidentally teach the day's skill, target behaviors, and the behaviors listed whether you use these activities or others. Remember that the dialogue provided in the session outlines (except for the lesson itself) is intended to be a model, not read or memorized verbatim. Read the dialogue over for main points and use your own spontaneous style. **Most of the dialogue and instructions are identical from skill to skill. For efficiency you may wish to attend only to the Relaxation Script number and the new information in the Skill Lesson.**

---

*Homework Completion and Free Play

In addition to today's skill and children's individual target behaviors, give special attention to taking responsibility, solving problems, and following directions (during Homework completion), and joining in, cooperating, problem solving, keeping a good attitude, and following directions (during free play).

Collect Homework and the bottom half of Home Notes; oversee free play and Homework completion or practice time.

Teacher 1:
(Scan papers to see which children have satisfactorily completed Homework; put aside Home Notes to check later.)

(children who completed it), you may go now and choose a game to play. (children who have not completed it), it's time for you to finish the Homework (or practice the skill) so that you can join the others.

(For children who habitually do not bring completed Homework, add more written questions or role play practice so that they finish about the same time as free play ends.)

Review Homework with children.

Teacher 1:
(Have children form a circle on the floor.)

Now let's look at the Homework you have done. I'm glad that (children who brought completed work) did their work at home. (a child who brought it), will you read your answer to Question _____?

(Have several children who brought their work read answers; ask for feedback from others. If you are using the Homework Progress Chart, allow children to color in the whole square or place a sticker in the square or color in part of it, depending on whether they brought completed Homework or finished it during free play.)

---

*Relaxation Training

In addition to today's skill and children's individual target behaviors, give special attention to keeping a calm body, solving problems, following directions, and keeping hands to self.

Lead relaxation training.

Teacher 1:
We are going to practice relaxing again. Relaxing will help you learn the new skill and help you face any problem.

(Have children find a place on the floor to lie down. Choose one child to turn off the lights.)

(Use Relaxation Script 4.)

Skill Lesson 10

● **Introduce skill and list components.**

Teacher 1:
Today we are going to talk about offering to help. To offer to help, you:
▪ Use a pleasant face and voice.
▪ Notice something that you can do for someone.
▪ Ask if you can help.
▪ If that person says "yes," then you do it.

. . . .

● **Role play appropriate example.**

Teacher 1:
This is the right way to offer to help. I'm outside on my bike when I notice mom drive up in the car, get out, and begin unloading groceries.
Hi, mom, can I help you unload the groceries?

Teacher 2:
Sure.

Teacher 1:
OK. (role plays helping)

● **Ask children for behavior components of skill.**

Teacher 1:
How did you know that was the right way to offer to help?
(children respond or are prompted)

● **Role play inappropriate example.**

Teacher 1:
This is the wrong way to offer to help. I'm outside on my bike when I notice mom drive up in the car, get out, and begin unloading groceries.
Hi, mom, I'm going for a bike ride!

● **Ask children for behavior components of skill.**

Teacher 1:
What should have happened to make that the right way to offer to help?
(children respond or are prompted)

. . . .

● **Ask children to role play.**

Teacher 1:
Now it is your turn to role play. (Assign role play situation.) I am going to call on someone who has been working really hard in the group by (specific on-task behaviors).
_____ has been working really hard the

whole time by (appropriate behaviors) and looks ready to be the first one to role play. _____, this is your role play.

(Describe the role play you have previously selected for this child from the role play sheet behind this session outline. Have each child role play the skill *correctly* at least one time.)

● **Ask children to give Positive Feedback.**

Teacher 1 or 2:
Good role playing. Who can give _____ *some Positive Feedback on his/her role play?*

(Call on child who is volunteering and paying attention.)

. . . .

● **Ask children for rationales for using skill.**

Teacher 1:
Why do you think it is important to offer to help?
(children respond or are prompted)

Children:
▪ People will offer to help you more often.
▪ Things get done faster.
▪ It's more fun to work together.

. . . .

● **Lead children through reality check.**

Teacher 1:
Sometimes you might try really hard to offer to help, *and this might happen.* I'm outside on my bike when I notice mom drive up in the car, get out, and begin unloading groceries.
Hi, mom, can I help you unload the groceries?

Teacher 2:
Well, it's about time you decided to do something around here! Here, you can unload all these groceries, and then you can put them away, and after that you can help me wash the vegetables and set the table, and get dinner ready.

Teacher 1:
You just did everything right to offer to help. *What should you do if this happens to you?*
(children respond or are prompted)

Children:
▪ Take a deep breath to get calm.
▪ Keep a good attitude.
▪ Keep offering to help.
▪ Ignore mom's bad attitude and follow her directions.

*Snack Time

In addition to today's skill and children's individual target behaviors, give special attention to following group rules, using conversation skills, cooperating, and solving problems.

Decide which children have earned all of snack.

Children may earn the entire snack or only a smaller portion if they join the snack in progress. Keep in mind how much difficulty a child has had following rules or practicing during the lesson and relaxation time to get an idea of how much time the child might need to practice to compensate for missed opportunities.

Dismiss children who have already earned snack time to the snack table.

Teacher 1:
OK, it's snack time now. (Teacher 2), who do you think has really been earning snack today?

Teacher 2:
Well, _____ has been really following the rules, having a still body, volunteering, and working on (his/her target behavior).

Teacher 1:
Yes, he/she really has. And I think _____ has also done a really good job of (specific behaviors). I'd like (child already named) to go to the snack table and pass out the napkins and (other child named) to go and pass out the cups.

(Continue dismissing children to the snack table by giving Positive Feedback for their accomplishments and assigning them a task at the snack table. If some children have not earned all of snack, have them practice as follows.)

Teacher 1:
_____, you need to sit here with me and practice (volunteering, keeping hands to self, etc.).

(Ask children questions from the lesson, have them role play, or do relaxation to give them opportunities to practice behaviors that were problematic during relaxation and/or the lesson. As the children practice, watch for a good attitude and effort in practicing and determine when each child seems to have made up for lost opportunities and achieved an acceptable level of competence in the skill or rule following.)

Ask children to clean up snack area.

Teacher 1:
OK, snack time is over now. We need to clean up. _____, would you get the garbage can and bring it around so everyone can throw away the garbage.

(Use Positive Feedback and other Teaching Strategies for cooperating and following directions during the cleanup.)

---

*Activity Time

In addition to today's skill and children's individual target behaviors, give special attention to following group rules, using conversation skills, cooperating, and solving problems.

Explain activity for today's lesson.

Teacher 1:
It's time for an activity now. Today we're going to (describe activity briefly). This is a time for us to practice our target behaviors and Offering to Help.

(Use Activity.)

Ask all the children to help clean up.

Teacher 1:
Now it's time for everyone to help clean up.

(Use Positive Feedback and other Teaching Strategies to help children work well together on cleanup. After cleanup, prompt children to return to circle.)

---

*Home Notes

In addition to today's skill and children's individual target behaviors, give special attention to following group rules and saying nice things.

Divide children into two groups and work on scoring Home Notes.

Teacher 1:
(a child), we are going to talk about how you did during today's session. Who can give (that child) some Positive Feedback and tell him/her good things about how he/she did on (target behavior)?

(Score the top half of the Home Note while the children are giving Positive Feedback. Ask for specific feedback for each of the child's target behaviors and add to it with comments you want to make, pointing out progress and areas needing improvement.)

(same child), now what do you think was the best thing you did in group today?
(child responds or is prompted)

Teacher 1:
That's good.

(Add specific descriptions of strong points.)

You might also try to (suggestions for improvement). Here is your Home Note.

(Repeat sequence with each child.)

---

*New Homework

In addition to today's skill and children's individual target behaviors, give special attention to following group rules and saying nice things.

Pass out Homework.

Teacher 1:
Here is your Homework. Be sure to do it and bring it back next time. Let's see what it says.

(Read aloud.)

If you need help, ask your parents or some other adult in your home.

Skill 10: Offering to Help
Role Plays

Situations / Target Behaviors	School Problems (Teacher/Peers)	Neighborhood Problems	Sibling Problems	Parent Problems
Listen Carefully	Your teacher mentions to the class that the janitor wants a volunteer to help him with a project.	You are at a friend's, and his mother says the two of you can continue playing only if he takes out the garbage.	You are watching T.V., and your sister says she'd like you to help her put her new bike together, but she has to do dishes now.	Your dad begins to clean the table after dinner and asks if anyone would walk to the store and get some ice cream.
Treat Others Nicely	A kid you don't like is on crutches and trying to carry his lunch box and library books.	An elderly man who lives near you is walking home with two bags of groceries. You were on your way to a friend's house.	Your little brother is trying to fix his broken toy spaceship and is not doing it right. You see what needs to be done.	Your mom is bringing in the groceries. There are a lot of bags.
Join in with Others	Your teacher says that the class will have a movie if the centers are cleaned up before recess. Several kids start.	Some kids in your neighborhood are collecting cans to recycle. You don't know if they like you or not.	Your sister is having a friend stay over and is working really hard to get her room ready. You want to play with them.	Your dad says he'd like to take everyone to a movie tonight, but he has to clean the house instead.
Keep a Good Attitude	You've done your share of cleaning the art table. The other two kids are goofing off. It has to be done before recess.	You are on your way to see a friend who is taking you to a movie which will start soon. Your neighbor asks you to help her.	Your mom asked you and your brother to clean the room. Your brother is complaining that it is mostly your mess.	Your mom comes home with a bunch of packages. She said she forgot to get the toy she had agreed to pick up for you.
Take Responsibility for Self	You accidently tear a page in a book. Later, you hear the teacher tell a kid who has it that she will have to pay a fine.	You are taking out the garbage, and the bag breaks. Papers blow down the street.	Your sister and you just finished a snack. She starts cleaning up. A friend of yours comes and wants you to play now.	Your dad drove you around for your paper route because it was raining. Now he is cleaning the garage.
Stay Calm and Relaxed	You see smoke coming out of the wastepaper basket while you're in the secretaries' office.	Your friend is borrowing your marbles and drops the jar. It breaks, and marbles roll down the street.	You are drinking some juice as you walk around the kitchen. You aren't looking, and you spill on your brother's homework.	You're having a surprise party for your dad. You want to watch for him, but the table needs to be set.
Solve Problems	You and some friends want to play baseball at recess, but there aren't any bases.	You want to play with two kids who live down the street. They are mowing and raking their lawn.	You want to ride bikes with your sister, but it is her turn to do dishes.	You need to bring some cookies to a party tomorrow. You're not sure how to do it, and your mom is busy weeding the garden.

Skill 10: Offering to Help
Activity

(This activity of making snacks can also be used with Skill 9: Sharing, Skill 11: Compromising, and Skill 13: Problem Solving. The activity provided for Skill 11: Compromising can also be used here with Skill 10.)

The materials needed are:

1. Ingredients for instant pudding, ice cream sundaes, doughnuts (from ready-made uncooked biscuits), etc. Choose a snack that will be practical, considering the children's age and skill level.
2. Bowls, teaspoons, measuring cups, serving spoons, electric skillet, etc., as needed for the snack chosen.

Discuss the procedure to be followed with the children. It may be helpful to write the recipe on the chalkboard. Making the snack may be approached as a "problem" that the children may solve, i.e., who will get to do what parts of the recipe.

Watch for Compromising, Offering to Help, Sharing, and Problem Solving. Use Positive Feedback for appropriate use of skills.

Skill 10: Offering to Help
Home Note

Name _____ Instructors _____

During today's lesson we practiced offering to help when we see that there is something we can do for someone else.

Today's Objectives	Target Behaviors

Today's Objectives

To offer to help, did the child:

	YES	NO
1. Use a pleasant face and voice?	___	___
2. Notice something that he/she could do for someone?	___	___
3. Ask if he/she could help?	___	___
4. Proceed to help the person, if the answer was "yes"?	___	___

Target Behaviors

Score

A. _____ _____
B. _____ _____
C. _____ _____
D. _____ _____
E. _____ _____

Score, using this scale:
1 = Completely satisfied
2 = Satisfied
3 = Slightly satisfied
4 = Neither satisfied nor dissatisfied
5 = Slightly dissatisfied
6 = Dissatisfied
7 = Completely dissatisfied

The best thing your child did today in social skills was _____

_____

- -

Parents – Please Complete This Section and Return
Skill 10: Offering to Help

Name _____

The following objectives and target behaviors refer to those named above. Please mark or score your child in these areas and have him/her return this bottom section with your signature to the next social skills group.

Did your child meet the objectives of today's lesson at least once this week?

	YES	NO
Objective 1	___	___
Objective 2	___	___
Objective 3	___	___
Objective 4	___	___

Score your child on his/her target behaviors, using the 1-7 scale above:

Target Behavior A _____

Target Behavior B _____

Target Behavior C _____

Target Behavior D _____

Target Behavior E _____

Parent Signature _____ Date _____

Skill 10: Offering to Help
Homework

Name _____

1. Write down two times you offered to help at home, school, or elsewhere this week.

   Time 1:

   a. Who did you help? _____

   _____

   b. Exactly what did you do? _____

   _____

   _____

   _____

   Time 2:

   a. Who did you help? _____

   _____

   b. Exactly what did you do? _____

   _____

   _____

   _____

2. Give two reasons why it is good to offer to help others.

   a. _____

   _____

   b. _____

   _____

3. Tell about a time someone offered to help you and how it made you feel.

   a. How did the person help? _____

   _____

   b. How did you feel? _____

   _____

Session 11

Skill 11: Compromising

YOU MAY SUBSTITUTE naturally occurring events (lunch time, art projects, etc.) for items marked with an asterisk. Be sure to incidentally teach the day's skill, target behaviors, and the behaviors listed whether you use these activities or others. Remember that the dialogue provided in the session outlines (except for the lesson itself) is intended to be a model, not read or memorized verbatim. Read the dialogue over for main points and use your own spontaneous style. **Most of the dialogue and instructions are identical from skill to skill. For efficiency you may wish to attend only to the Relaxation Script number and the new information in the Skill Lesson.**

---

*Homework Completion and Free Play

In addition to today's skill and children's individual target behaviors, give special attention to taking responsibility, solving problems, and following directions (during Homework completion), and joining in, cooperating, problem solving, keeping a good attitude, and following directions (during free play).

Collect Homework and the bottom half of Home Notes; oversee free play and Homework completion or practice time.

Teacher 1:
(Scan papers to see which children have satisfactorily completed Homework; put aside Home Notes to check later.)

(children who completed it), you may go now and choose a game to play. (children who have not completed it), it's time for you to finish the Homework (or practice the skill) so that you can join the others.

(For children who habitually do not bring completed Homework, add more written questions or role play practice so that they finish about the same time as free play ends.)

Review Homework with children.

Teacher 1:
(Have children form a circle on the floor.)

Now let's look at the Homework you have done. I'm glad that (children who brought completed work) did their work at home. (a child who brought it), will you read your answer to Question _____?

(Have several children who brought their work read answers; ask for feedback from others. If you are using the Homework Progress Chart, allow children to color in the whole square or place a sticker in the square or color in part of it, depending on whether they brought completed Homework or finished it during free play.)

---

*Relaxation Training

In addition to today's skill and children's individual target behaviors, give special attention to keeping a calm body, solving problems, following directions, and keeping hands to self.

Lead relaxation training.

Teacher 1:
We are going to practice relaxing again. Relaxing will help you learn the new skill and help you face any problem.

(Have children find a place on the floor to lie down. Choose one child to turn off the lights.)

(Use Relaxation Script 4.)

Skill Lesson 11

● Introduce skill and list components.

Teacher 1:
Today we are going to talk about compromising. Compromising is figuring out how you, as well as others, can all get something you want, when it seems that everybody wants something different. To compromise, you:
▪ Use a pleasant face and voice.
▪ Think of a way both people can get something that they want.
▪ Suggest it.

. . . .

● Role play appropriate example.

Teacher 1:
This is the right way to compromise. I'm jumping rope in my yard, and my friend comes over on his bicycle.

Teacher 2:
Hi, do you want to play?

Teacher 1:
Yeah, let's jump rope together.

Teacher 2:
No, let's ride bikes.

Teacher 1:
Well, why don't we ride bikes for a while, and then jump rope later?

Teacher 2:
OK.

● Ask children for behavior components of skill.

Teacher 1:
How did you know that was the right way to compromise?
(children respond or are prompted)

● Role play inappropriate example.

Teacher 1:
This is the wrong way to compromise. I'm jumping rope in my yard, and my friend comes over on his bicycle.

Teacher 2:
Hi, do you want to play?

Teacher 1:
Yeah, let's jump rope together.

Teacher 2:
No, let's ride bikes.

Teacher 1:
Well, I guess we can't play together then.

● Ask children for behavior components of skill.

Teacher 1:
What should have happened to make that the right way to compromise?
(children respond or are prompted)

. . . .

● Ask children to role play.

Teacher 1:
Now it is your turn to role play. (Assign role play situation.) I am going to call on someone who has been working really hard in the group by (specific on-task behaviors). _____ has been working really hard the whole time by (appropriate behaviors) and looks ready to be the first one to role play. _____, this is your role play.

(Describe the role play you have previously selected for this child from the role play sheet behind this session outline. Have each child role play the skill *correctly* at least one time.)

● Ask children to give Positive Feedback.

Teacher 1 or 2:
Good role playing. Who can give _____ *some Positive Feedback on his/her role play?*

(Call on child who is volunteering and paying attention.)

. . . .

● Ask children for rationales for using skill.

Teacher 1:
Why do you think it is important to compromise?
(children respond or are prompted)

Children:
▪ Others feel better about being with you.
▪ Others will try to compromise with you.
▪ Everyone gets a little of what he/she wants.

. . . .

● Lead children through reality check.

Teacher 1:
Sometimes you might try really hard to compromise, *and this might happen.* I'm jumping rope in my yard, and my friend comes over on his bicycle.

Teacher 2:
Hi, do you want to play?

Teacher 1:
Yeah, let's jump rope together.

Teacher 2:
No, let's ride bikes.

Teacher 1:
Well, why don't we ride bikes for a while, and then jump rope later?

Teacher 2:
No, let's just ride bikes. I don't want to do anything else.

Teacher 1:
You just did everything right to compromise. *What should you do if this happens to you?*
(children respond or are prompted)

Children:
- Take a deep breath to get calm.
- Keep a good attitude.
- Try to compromise again later.
- Go find someone else to play with.

---

*Snack Time

In addition to today's skill and children's individual target behaviors, give special attention to following group rules, using conversation skills, cooperating, and solving problems.

Decide which children have earned all of snack.

Children may earn the entire snack or only a smaller portion if they join the snack in progress. Keep in mind how much difficulty a child has had following rules or practicing during the lesson and relaxation time to get an idea of how much time the child might need to practice to compensate for missed opportunities.

Dismiss children who have already earned snack time to the snack table.

Teacher 1:
OK, it's snack time now. (Teacher 2), who do you think has really been earning snack today?

Teacher 2:
Well, _____ has been really following the rules, having a still body, volunteering, and working on (his/her target behavior).

Teacher 1:
Yes, he/she really has. And I think _____ has also done a really good job of (specific behaviors). I'd like (child already named) to go to the snack table and pass out the napkins and (other child named) to go and pass out the cups.

(Continue dismissing children to the snack table by giving Positive Feedback for their accomplishments and assigning them a task at the snack table. If some children have not earned all of snack, have them practice as follows.)

Teacher 1:
_____, you need to sit here with me and practice (volunteering, keeping hands to self, etc.).

(Ask children questions from the lesson, have them role play, or do relaxation to give them opportunities to practice behaviors that were problematic during relaxation and/or the lesson. As the children practice, watch for a good attitude and effort in practicing and determine when each child seems to have made up for lost opportunities and achieved an acceptable level of competence in the skill or rule following.)

Ask children to clean up snack area.

Teacher 1:
OK, snack time is over now. We need to clean up. _____, would you get the garbage can and bring it around so everyone can throw away the garbage.

(Use Positive Feedback and other Teaching Strategies for cooperating and following directions during the cleanup.)

---

*Activity Time

In addition to today's skill and children's individual target behaviors, give special attention to following group rules, using conversation skills, cooperating, and solving problems.

Explain activity for today's lesson.

Teacher 1:
It's time for an activity now. Today we're going to (describe activity briefly). This is a time for us to practice our target behaviors and Compromising.

(Use Activity.)

Ask all the children to help clean up.

Teacher 1:
Now it's time for everyone to help clean up.

(Use Positive Feedback and other Teaching Strategies to help children work well together on cleanup. After cleanup, prompt children to return to circle.)

---

*Home Notes

In addition to today's skill and children's individual target behaviors, give special attention to following group rules and saying nice things.

Divide children into two groups and work on scoring Home Notes.

Teacher 1:
(a child), we are going to talk about how you did during today's session. Who can give (that child) some Positive Feedback and tell him/her good things about how he/she did on (target behavior)?

(Score the top half of the Home Note while the children are giving Positive Feedback. Ask for specific feedback for each of the child's target behaviors and add to it with comments you want to make, pointing out progress and areas needing improvement.)

(same child), now what do you think was the best thing you did in group today?
(child responds or is prompted)

Teacher 1:
That's good.

(Add specific descriptions of strong points.)

You might also try to (suggestions for improvement). Here is your Home Note.

(Repeat sequence with each child.)

---

*New Homework

In addition to today's skill and children's individual target behaviors, give special attention to following group rules and saying nice things.

Pass out Homework.

Teacher 1:
Here is your Homework. Be sure to do it and bring it back next time. Let's see what it says.

(Read aloud.)

If you need help, ask your parents or some other adult in your home.

Skill 11: Compromising
Role Plays

Situations / Target Behaviors	School Problems (Teacher/Peers)	Neighborhood Problems	Sibling Problems	Parent Problems
Listen Carefully	Your teacher is assigning special jobs for a class project. By mistake she assigns two of you the same job.	You and a friend can get one pizza. Your friend likes pepperoni, but you want sausage.	Your mom asks what you would like for dessert. You want ice cream; your sister wants cake. You can have only one thing.	Mom gives you many jobs to do as she gets ready to leave. You're afraid you can't finish them all by the time she returns.
Treat Others Nicely	The winner of the spelling bee gets to choose the P.E. activity. When time is up, two of you are tied for first place.	A bunch of kids in your neighborhood get together for a basketball game, but there is one extra person.	You and your sister go in the family room to watch T.V. Your sister wants to sit in the comfortable chair, and so do you.	You ask your mom if she will take you swimming. She says she will, but she's doing the dishes right now.
Join in with Others	You are the team captain today. Two people on your team want to be the pitcher. You need to help settle the matter.	Your friend comes over to play. Your friend wants to ride bikes, but you want to play catch.	You and your brother are doing the yard. The jobs are weeding the garden and mowing the lawn. You both want to mow.	Your family plans to camp with friends who live far away. Dad doesn't want to drive that far; you know of a good place half way.
Keep a Good Attitude	You have some free time during class to play a game. Your friend wants to play "Battleship," but you want to play checkers.	You go to your friend's house to go swimming. When you get there, your friend has decided to watch T.V. instead.	You and your brother both want to sit in the front seat of the car on the way to the store. Only one of you can fit.	One of your favorite T.V. shows is just starting, but your parents come in and want to watch the news.
Take Responsibility for Self	You are on the playground with your friend. Your friend wants to join the dodgeball game, but you want to play four-square.	You're babysitting. The two children start arguing about what game to play. You need to help settle the matter.	If you and your sister finish vacuuming and washing the windows, you can go out for ice cream. You both want to vacuum.	You go shopping with your mom. You like an outfit that costs $30; mom has $20 for you to spend. You have $20 saved up.
Stay Calm and Relaxed	For a class project you are baking cookies. You and a classmate want to use the cookie cutter at the same time.	You're staying at your friend's house. You want to go out and play. Your friend says he has to do his chore, folding laundry.	You go and turn on the T.V. You want to watch one show, but your brother wants to watch another.	Your parents say you spend too much time playing sports; you *have to* learn to play an instrument. Mom prefers the harp.
Solve Problems	Your teacher has told you and a classmate that you can each take out a ball today. You discover that one of the balls is flat.	You and a friend go to the movies. When you both get there, you want to see one movie, but your friend wants to see a different one.	You and your brother have just finished building a model plane. You both want to put it in your own room.	Your mom is making chocolate chip cookies. She likes to put walnuts in them, but you don't like walnuts.

99

Skill 11: Compromising
Activity

(This activity called Drawing Pictures Together can also be used with Skill 9: Sharing and Skill 10: Offering to Help.)

The materials needed are:
1. Crayons, paints, and/or markers (one set for each group of children).
2. Construction paper of different colors.
3. Scissors (*one* pair).
4. Glue (*one* bottle).

At the beginning of the activity, divide the children up into groups of two or three. Explain that each group will be making a picture. The picture may represent a monster, or a robot they would like to have in their homes, or a house in which they would like to live, etc. The group *as a whole* must decide what their monster, or animal, robot, etc. will look like, e.g., its color and shape. Each group must share one set of crayons, paints, or markers. All the groups must share the scissors and glue.

Watch for examples of Sharing, Compromising, and Offering to Help. Give Positive Feedback. When necessary, intervene. Using the Teaching Interaction or any other appropriate Teaching Strategy, help the children to practice the skills.

Skill 11: Compromising
Home Note

Name _____ Instructors _____

During today's lesson we practiced compromising. When it seemed that everyone wanted something different, we thought of a compromise, that is, a way in which each person could get something that he/she wanted.

Today's Objectives			Target Behaviors	
To compromise, did the child:				Score
	YES	NO	A. _____	_____
1. Use a pleasant face and voice?	_____	_____	B. _____	_____
2. Think of a way both people could get something that they want?	_____	_____	C. _____	_____
			D. _____	_____
3. Suggest it?	_____	_____	E. _____	_____

Score, using this scale:
1 = Completely satisfied
2 = Satisfied
3 = Slightly satisfied
4 = Neither satisfied nor dissatisfied
5 = Slightly dissatisfied
6 = Dissatisfied
7 = Completely dissatisfied

The best thing your child did today in social skills was _____
_____

- -

Parents – Please Complete This Section and Return
Skill 11: Compromising

Name _____

The following objectives and target behaviors refer to those named above. Please mark or score your child in these areas and have him/her return this bottom section with your signature to the next social skills group.

Did your child meet the objectives of today's lesson at least once this week?			Score your child on his/her target behaviors, using the 1-7 scale above:
	YES	NO	
Objective 1	_____	_____	Target Behavior A _____
Objective 2	_____	_____	Target Behavior B _____
Objective 3	_____	_____	Target Behavior C _____
			Target Behavior D _____
			Target Behavior E _____

Parent Signature _____ Date _____

Skill 11: Compromising
Homework

Name _____

1. Write down two times you compromised with somebody else so that you both were able to get something that you wanted.

   Time 1:

   a. What was the problem? _____

   _____

   b. What was the compromise you thought of? _____

   _____

   _____

   _____

   Time 2:

   a. What was the problem? _____

   _____

   b. What was the compromise you thought of? _____

   _____

   _____

   _____

2. Give two reasons why it is good to compromise.

   a. _____

   _____

   b. _____

   _____

3. What are three things you could do if you tried to compromise, but the other person would not?

   a. _____

   _____

   b. _____

   _____

   c. _____

   _____

Session 12

Skill 12: Asking for Clear Directions

YOU MAY SUBSTITUTE naturally occurring events (lunch time, art projects, etc.) for items marked with an asterisk. Be sure to incidentally teach the day's skill, target behaviors, and the behaviors listed whether you use these activities or others. Remember that the dialogue provided in the session outlines (except for the lesson itself) is intended to be a model, not read or memorized verbatim. Read the dialogue over for main points and use your own spontaneous style. **Most of the dialogue and instructions are identical from skill to skill. For efficiency you may wish to attend only to the Relaxation Script number and the new information in the Skill Lesson.**

---

*Homework Completion and Free Play

In addition to today's skill and children's individual target behaviors, give special attention to taking responsibility, solving problems, and following directions (during Homework completion), and joining in, cooperating, problem solving, keeping a good attitude, and following directions (during free play).

Collect Homework and the bottom half of Home Notes; oversee free play and Homework completion or practice time.

Teacher 1:
(Scan papers to see which children have satisfactorily completed Homework; put aside Home Notes to check later.)

(children who completed it), you may go now and choose a game to play. (children who have not completed it), it's time for you to finish the Homework (or practice the skill) so that you can join the others.

(For children who habitually do not bring completed Homework, add more written questions or role play practice so that they finish about the same time as free play ends.)

Review Homework with children.

Teacher 1:
(Have children form a circle on the floor.)

Now let's look at the Homework you have done. I'm glad that (children who brought completed work) did their work at home. (a child who brought it), will you read your answer to Question _____?

(Have several children who brought their work read answers; ask for feedback from others. If you are using the Homework Progress Chart, allow children to color in the whole square or place a sticker in the square or color in part of it, depending on whether they brought completed Homework or finished it during free play.)

---

*Relaxation Training

In addition to today's skill and children's individual target behaviors, give special attention to keeping a calm body, solving problems, following directions, and keeping hands to self.

Lead relaxation training.

Teacher 1:
We are going to practice relaxing again. Relaxing will help you learn the new skill and help you face any problem.

(Have children find a place on the floor to lie down. Choose one child to turn off the lights.)

(Use Relaxation Script 5.)

Skill Lesson 12

● Introduce skill and list components.

Teacher 1:

Today we are going to talk about asking for clear directions. When someone gives you directions you don't understand, you should ask for clear directions. To ask for clear directions, you:

▪ Use a pleasant face and voice.
▪ Look at the person.
▪ Ask for more information.
▪ Repeat the directions to the person.

. . . .

● Role play appropriate example.

Teacher 1:

This is the right way to ask for clear directions. I'm with my dad, and he wants me to clean out the garage.

Teacher 2:

_____, I'd like you to clean out the garage.

Teacher 1:

OK. What exactly would you like me to do?

Teacher 2:

I want you to stack the wood in a pile, empty the cat box, and put the toys in the toy box.

Teacher 1:

OK. You want me to stack the wood, empty the cat box, and put the toys in the toy box.

Teacher 2:

That's right.

● Ask children for behavior components of skill.

Teacher 1:

How did you know that was the right way to ask for clear directions?
(children respond or are prompted)

● Role play inappropriate example.

Teacher 1:

This is the wrong way to ask for clear directions. I'm with my dad, and he wants me to clean out the garage.

Teacher 2:

_____, I'd like you to clean out the garage.

Teacher 1:

OK. I'll do it right away.

● Ask children for behavior components of skill.

Teacher 1:

What should have happened to make that the right way to

ask for clear directions?
(children respond or are prompted)

. . . .

● Ask children to role play.

Teacher 1:

Now it is your turn to role play. (Assign role play situation.) I am going to call on someone who has been working really hard in the group by (specific on-task behaviors). _____ has been working really hard the whole time by (appropriate behaviors) and looks ready to be the first one to role play. _____, this is your role play.

(Describe the role play you have previously selected for this child from the role play sheet behind this session outline. Have each child role play the skill *correctly* at least one time.)

● Ask children to give Positive Feedback.

Teacher 1 or 2:

Good role playing. Who can give _____ *some Positive Feedback on his/her role play?*

(Call on child who is volunteering and paying attention.)

. . . .

● Ask children for rationales for using skill.

Teacher 1:

Why do you think it is important to ask for clear directions?
(children respond or are prompted)

Children:

▪ Makes communication smoother; people get along better when they understand what is expected.
▪ When you don't understand something and you get more information, it is easier to complete tasks.
▪ You get along better with parents, teachers, and peers.
▪ If you repeat what is said, you decrease chances of misunderstanding.
▪ You feel better about yourself because you do what is asked without mistakes.

. . . .

● Lead children through reality check.

Teacher 1:

Sometimes you might try really hard to ask for clear directions, *and this might happen.* I'm with my dad, and he wants me to clean out the garage.

Teacher 2:

_____, I'd like you to clean out the garage.

Teacher 1:
OK. What exactly would you like me to do?

Teacher 2:
I told you to go clean it out! You'll see the mess in there; clean it up!

Teacher 1:
You just did everything right to ask for clear directions. *What should you do if this happens to you?*

(children respond or are prompted)

Children:
- Take a deep breath to get calm.
- Keep a good attitude.
- Do the best you can on the basis of what you heard.
- Explain to the person that you are not sure what he/she means.
- Try again later to ask for clear directions.

---

*Snack Time

In addition to today's skill and children's individual target behaviors, give special attention to following group rules, using conversation skills, cooperating, and solving problems.

Decide which children have earned all of snack.

Children may earn the entire snack or only a smaller portion if they join the snack in progress. Keep in mind how much difficulty a child has had following rules or practicing during the lesson and relaxation time to get an idea of how much time the child might need to practice to compensate for missed opportunities.

Dismiss children who have already earned snack time to the snack table.

Teacher 1:
OK, it's snack time now. (Teacher 2), who do you think has really been earning snack today?

Teacher 2:
Well, _____ has been really following the rules, having a still body, volunteering, and working on (his/her target behavior).

Teacher 1:
Yes, he/she really has. And I think _____ has also done a really good job of (specific behaviors). I'd like (child already named) to go to the snack table and pass out the napkins and (other child named) to go and pass out the cups.

(Continue dismissing children to the snack table by giving Positive Feedback for their accomplishments and assigning them a task at the snack table. If some children have not earned all of snack, have them practice as follows.)

Teacher 1:
_____, you need to sit here with me and practice (volunteering, keeping hands to self, etc.).

(Ask children questions from the lesson, have them role play, or do relaxation to give them opportunities to practice behaviors that were problematic during relaxation and/or the lesson. As the children practice, watch for a good attitude and effort in practicing and determine when each child seems to have made up for lost opportunities and achieved an acceptable level of competence in the skill or rule following.)

Ask children to clean up snack area.

Teacher 1:
OK, snack time is over now. We need to clean up. _____, would you get the garbage can and bring it around so everyone can throw away the garbage.

(Use Positive Feedback and other Teaching Strategies for cooperating and following directions during the cleanup.)

---

*Activity Time

In addition to today's skill and children's individual target behaviors, give special attention to following group rules, using conversation skills, cooperating, and solving problems.

Explain activity for today's lesson.

Teacher 1:
It's time for an activity now. Today we're going to (describe activity briefly). This is a time for us to practice our target behaviors and Asking for Clear Directions.

(Use Activity.)

Ask all the children to help clean up.

Teacher 1:
Now it's time for everyone to help clean up.

(Use Positive Feedback and other Teaching Strategies to help children work well together on cleanup. After cleanup, prompt children to return to circle.)

---

*Home Notes

In addition to today's skill and children's individual target behaviors, give special attention to following group rules and saying nice things.

Divide children into two groups and work on scoring Home Notes.

Teacher 1:
(a child), we are going to talk about how you did during today's session. Who can give (that child) some Positive Feedback and tell him/her good things about how he/she did on (target behavior)?

(Score the top half of the Home Note while the children are giving Positive Feedback. Ask for specific feedback for each of the child's target behaviors and add to it with comments you want to make, pointing out progress and areas needing improvement.)

(same child), now what do you think was the best thing you did in group today?
(child responds or is prompted)

Teacher 1:
That's good.

(Add specific descriptions of strong points.)

You might also try to (suggestions for improvement). Here is your Home Note.

(Repeat sequence with each child.)

---

*New Homework

In addition to today's skill and children's individual target behaviors, give special attention to following group rules and saying nice things.

Pass out Homework.

Teacher 1:
Here is your Homework. Be sure to do it and bring it back next time. Let's see what it says.

(Read aloud.)

If you need help, ask your parents or some other adult in your home.

Relaxation Script 5

(This script may be used in conjunction with Skills 12 and 13. Please review the section on relaxation training in Chapter 5 of the Guide.)

Today we're going to practice how to relax our bodies and keep calm by taking slow, deep breaths.

As I count to three, breathe in slowly, and as you breathe out, think to yourself "I AM CALM." (count aloud slowly) One . . . two . . . three. (pause) Relax. Did you feel your stomach fill up with air? Notice how your body feels more relaxed and how calm you feel. (pause) As you take a slow, deep breath and let it go, you are letting out tensions and worries.

Now think about your face. If your forehead, mouth, or eyes feel tense, relax them, and let your face go smooth. (pause) As I count to three, take a deep breath, and as you breathe out, think the words "I AM CALM." (count aloud slowly) One . . . two . . . three. (pause) Relax.

Now think about your shoulders. If they feel tight, let them go soft and loose. (pause) As I count to three, breathe in slowly, and as you breathe out, think the words "I AM CALM." (count aloud slowly) One . . . two . . . three.(pause) Relax.

Now think about your arms and hands. If they feel tight, relax them, and let them flop loosely and quietly at your sides. As I count to three, take a deep breath, and as you breathe out, think the words "I AM CALM." (count aloud slowly) One . . . two . . . three. (pause) Relax.

Think about your stomach. If it feels tight, let it go soft. (pause) As I count to three, breathe in slowly, and as you breathe out, think the words "I AM CALM." (count aloud slowly) One . . . two . . . three. (pause) Relax.

Now think about your legs and feet. If they feel tight, relax them and let them flop softly and quietly on the floor. (pause) As I count to three, breathe in slowly, and as you breathe out, think the words "I AM CALM." (count aloud slowly) One . . . two . . . three. (pause) Relax.

Now that you are relaxed, imagine that you have a problem. Let's say that you left your lunch money at home. You feel hungry, and you don't have any extra money. Your body feels upset and angry. Think about how your body feels; your stomach and face may feel tense. (pause) If they are feeling tense, let them go soft. As I count to three, breathe in slowly, and as you breathe out, think the words "I AM CALM." (count aloud slowly) One . . . two . . . three. (pause) Relax.

One more time, keep your body loose and relaxed and think of that time you had a problem that was hard to solve. (pause) As I count to three, breathe in slowly, and as you breathe out, think the words "I AM CALM." (count aloud slowly) One . . . two . . . three. (pause) Relax. You feel so much better now that your body feels calm.

Now I want you to think of the last time you had a problem. (pause and give children a chance to think of their own situations) Imagine yourself in this situation. Think about how your body feels. Your stomach is upset; your face and arms are tense. If your body feels tight, let it go soft and relaxed. (pause) As I count to three, breathe in slowly, and as you breathe out, think the words "I AM CALM." (count aloud slowly) One . . . two . . . three. (pause) Relax. One more time, keep your body loose and relaxed and think of that time you had a problem. (pause) As I count to three, breathe in slowly, and as you breathe out, think the words "I AM CALM." (count aloud slowly) One . . . two . . . three. (pause) Relax.

Now your body feels calm and relaxed. The next time you have a problem and begin to feel upset, sad, or angry, remember to take a slow deep breath and relax your body; then you will be able to solve your problem more easily.

Skill 12: Asking for Clear Directions
Role Plays

Situations / Target Behaviors	School Problems (Teacher/Peers)	Neighborhood Problems	Sibling Problems	Parent Problems
Listen Carefully	You have finished all your assignments. Your teacher asks you to set up the special snack she has prepared.	Your neighbor asks you to water his lawn while he is on vacation.	Your sister asks you to get her jacket.	Your dad asks you to do the yard work today.
Treat Others Nicely	Your teacher asks you to take the new kid around school and show her where things are.	The older woman who lives next door sees you and asks, "Could you please come over and help me plant my flowers?"	Your brother is going to camp for a week and asks if you will do his chores for him while he's gone.	Your mom says, "Take care of the laundry before you go out to play."
Join in with Others	It's your first day at a new school. The principal tells you your classroom is #32. You don't know where that is.	You're at a friend's house and she says, "You make some lemonade, and I'll get out the cookies."	Your sister asks, "Will you help me clean up the kitchen?"	Dad is helping you fix your bicycle tire and says, "Will you get the stuff to fix the tire?"
Keep a Good Attitude	Your social skills teacher tells you, "You need to work on being a good listener."	Your dog got out and dug up the neighbor's flower garden. Your neighbor says, "You'll have to repair the damage."	Your mom tells you, "Please help your little brother get ready to go out to dinner."	Your mom says, "I'd like you to help me clean up the bathrooms."
Take Responsibility for Self	Your teacher gives you directions: "Go to the office, ask the secretary for the testing materials, and bring them back."	Your babysitter tells you to clean up the family room really well.	You are helping your brother clean out the garage, and he says, "Move those boxes."	Your dad says, "If you behave this afternoon, we can go to the movies tonight."
Stay Calm and Relaxed	Your teacher says, "You are in charge of closing up the room whenever we all leave it."	Your friend asks you to feed his dog because he's going to be gone this weekend.	Your mom and dad are gone. Your big sister is in charge. You're going to a friend's house; she says, "Be home early."	Your mom says, "I want you to clean up the mess in your room."
Solve Problems	Your teacher gives the class a math assignment but forgets to tell you the page number.	Your neighbor asks, "Will you take care of my house? I'll be gone next week." She names several jobs.	Your dad says, "You need to be nicer to your little sister."	Your mom says, "I'd like you to go to the store to get some groceries." She gives you a long list.

Skill 12: Asking for Clear Directions
Activity

(The activity provided for Skill 9: Sharing can also be used here with Skill 12.)

The materials needed are:

1. Small prizes and candy or fruit treats.
2. Bags for children to put their prizes in.
3. Rules board.

Hide the prizes before the children arrive. When it is time for the activity, explain that the game for the day will be a treasure hunt.

The rules are:

1. Each child must hunt only within the area assigned to him/her.
2. There is a time limit.
3. Each person can get a bag to hold the things he/she finds.

Note that the rules are stated vaguely and the prizes are not described. Watch for and give Positive Feedback for examples of Asking for Clear Directions. If none of the children ask for clarification, help them by asking, "Do you understand?" and by more structured and explicit prompts if they still fail to ask for clearer directions.

For extra practice, you may want to distribute lists of clues to each child. The clues should be very vaguely stated. If children ask for clarification without interrupting, you may answer their questions (whispering to the individual child or handing him/her slips of paper with more detailed clues). You may want to prompt this by telling them they may talk to you during the game or by explaining that you will provide more information to those who ask for clear directions appropriately.

Skill 12: Asking for Clear Directions
Home Note

Name _____ Instructors _____

During today's lesson we practiced asking for clear directions, that is, asking for more information when a person gives us directions that we don't understand. Included in this is repeating the directions to the person to make sure we understand correctly.

Today's Objectives	Target Behaviors

Today's Objectives

To ask for clear directions, did the child:

	YES	NO
1. Use a pleasant face and voice?	___	___
2. Look at the person?	___	___
3. Ask for more information?	___	___
4. Repeat the directions to the person?	___	___

Target Behaviors

Score

A. _____ ____
B. _____ ____
C. _____ ____
D. _____ ____
E. _____ ____

Score, using this scale:
1 = Completely satisfied
2 = Satisfied
3 = Slightly satisfied
4 = Neither satisfied nor dissatisfied
5 = Slightly dissatisfied
6 = Dissatisfied
7 = Completely dissatisfied

The best thing your child did today in social skills was _____

_____

- -

Parents – Please Complete This Section and Return
Skill 12: Asking for Clear Directions

Name _____

The following objectives and target behaviors refer to those named above. Please mark or score your child in these areas and have him/her return this bottom section with your signature to the next social skills group.

Did your child meet the objectives of today's lesson at least once this week?

	YES	NO
Objective 1	___	___
Objective 2	___	___
Objective 3	___	___
Objective 4	___	___

Score your child on his/her target behaviors, using the 1-7 scale above:

Target Behavior A _____
Target Behavior B _____
Target Behavior C _____
Target Behavior D _____
Target Behavior E _____

Parent Signature _____ Date _____

Skill 12: Asking for Clear Directions
Homework

Name _____

1. Write down two different directions someone gave you that you did not understand. Write down what you said and did and what the other person said and did for each one.

Direction 1:

a. What was the direction? _____

_____

b. What did you do and say? _____

_____

c. What did the other person do and say? _____

_____

Direction 2:

a. What was the direction? _____

_____

b. What did you do and say? _____

_____

c. What did the other person do and say? _____

_____

2. Give two reasons why it is important to ask for clear directions when you do not understand.

a. _____

_____

b. _____

_____

Session 13

Skill 13: Problem Solving

YOU MAY SUBSTITUTE naturally occurring events (lunch time, art projects, etc.) for items marked with an asterisk. Be sure to incidentally teach the day's skill, target behaviors, and the behaviors listed whether you use these activities or others. Remember that the dialogue provided in the session outlines (except for the lesson itself) is intended to be a model, not read or memorized verbatim. Read the dialogue over for main points and use your own spontaneous style. **Most of the dialogue and instructions are identical from skill to skill. For efficiency you may wish to attend only to the Relaxation Script number and the new information in the Skill Lesson.**

---

*Homework Completion and Free Play

In addition to today's skill and children's individual target behaviors, give special attention to taking responsibility, solving problems, and following directions (during Homework completion), and joining in, cooperating, problem solving, keeping a good attitude, and following directions (during free play).

Collect Homework and the bottom half of Home Notes; oversee free play and Homework completion or practice time.

Teacher 1:
(Scan papers to see which children have satisfactorily completed Homework; put aside Home Notes to check later.)

(children who completed it), you may go now and choose a game to play. (children who have not completed it), it's time for you to finish the Homework (or practice the skill) so that you can join the others.

(For children who habitually do not bring completed Homework, add more written questions or role play practice so that they finish about the same time as free play ends.)

Review Homework with children.

Teacher 1:
(Have children form a circle on the floor.)

Now let's look at the Homework you have done. I'm glad that (children who brought completed work) did their work at home. (a child who brought it), will you read your answer to Question _____?

(Have several children who brought their work read answers; ask for feedback from others. If you are using the Homework Progress Chart, allow children to color in the whole square or place a sticker in the square or color in part of it, depending on whether they brought completed Homework or finished it during free play.)

---

*Relaxation Training

In addition to today's skill and children's individual target behaviors, give special attention to keeping a calm body, solving problems, following directions, and keeping hands to self.

Lead relaxation training.

Teacher 1:
We are going to practice relaxing again. Relaxing will help you learn the new skill and help you face any problem.

(Have children find a place on the floor to lie down. Choose one child to turn off the lights.)

(Use Relaxation Script 5.)

Skill Lesson 13

● Introduce skill and list components.

Teacher 1:
Today we are going to talk about solving problems. A problem is a situation that makes you feel bad. Once you have a problem, you can either do things to make the problem worse for you, or you can do things to make it better for you, that is, solve it. To make a problem better and solve it, you:
- Take a deep breath to get a calm body and good attitude.
- Think of at least three different things you can do.
- Pick the best one for you.
- Try that one first.

. . . .

● Role play appropriate example.

Teacher 1:
This is the right way to solve a problem. When I get to school in the morning, I realize that I have forgotten my lunch money.
Boy, I sure feel like crying, but that won't help me get lunch, so I'll take a deep breath to get calm and think of three different things I can do to solve the problem. Let's see, I could ask to call my mom to see if she'll bring me the money. Or, I could ask a friend if I could borrow some money. Or, I could ask the principal if I could pay for my lunch tomorrow. I think I'll try calling my mom first, and if that doesn't work, I'll try something else.

● Ask children for behavior components of skill.

Teacher 1:
How did you know that was the right way to solve a problem?
(children respond or are prompted)

● Role play inappropriate example.

Teacher 1:
This is the wrong way to solve a problem. When I get to school in the morning, I realize that I have forgotten my lunch money. Oh no, what am I going to do?! Boo hoo! (role plays crying)

● Ask children for behavior components of skill.

Teacher 1:
What should have happened to make that the right way to solve a problem?

(children respond or are prompted)
. . . .

● Ask children to role play.

Teacher 1:
Now it is your turn to role play. (Assign role play situation.) I am going to call on someone who has been working really hard in the group by (specific on-task behaviors). _____ has been working really hard the whole time by (appropriate behaviors) and looks ready to be the first one to role play. _____, this is your role play.

(Describe the role play you have previously selected for this child from the role play sheet behind this session outline. Have each child role play the skill *correctly* at least one time.)

● Ask children to give Positive Feedback.

Teacher 1 or 2:
Good role playing. Who can give _____ *some Positive Feedback on his/her role play?*

(Call on child who is volunteering and paying attention.)
. . . .

● Ask children for rationales for using skill.

Teacher 1:
Why do you think it is important to know how to solve your problems?
(children respond or are prompted)

Children:
- You won't have to wait for others to solve your problems for you.
- You will feel better.
- Things will be easier.
- You will get into less trouble.

. . . .

● Lead children through reality check.

Teacher 1:
Sometimes you might try really hard to solve a problem, *and this might happen.* When I get to school in the morning, I realize that I have forgotten my lunch money.
Boy, I sure feel like crying, but that won't help me get lunch, so I'll take a deep breath to get calm and think of three different things I can do to solve the problem. Let's see, I could ask to call my mom to see if she'll bring me the money. Or, I could ask a friend if I could borrow some money. Or, I could ask the principal if I could pay for my lunch tomorrow. I think I'll try calling my mom first, and if that doesn't work, I'll try something else.

Hello, mom. I forgot my lunch money. Would you bring it, please?

Teacher 2:
No, you're always forgetting things. You can just go without lunch today!

Teacher 1:
Bye, mom.

Teacher 1:
You just did everything right to try to solve your problem. What should you do if this happens to you?
(children respond or are prompted)

Children:
- Take a deep breath to get calm.
- Keep a good attitude.
- Try another solution.

---

*Snack Time

In addition to today's skill and children's individual target behaviors, give special attention to following group rules, using conversation skills, cooperating, and solving problems.

Decide which children have earned all of snack.

Children may earn the entire snack or only a smaller portion if they join the snack in progress. Keep in mind how much difficulty a child has had following rules or practicing during the lesson and relaxation time to get an idea of how much time the child might need to practice to compensate for missed opportunities.

Dismiss children who have already earned snack time to the snack table.

Teacher 1:
OK, it's snack time now. (Teacher 2), who do you think has really been earning snack today?

Teacher 2:
Well, _____ has been really following the rules, having a still body, volunteering, and working on (his/her target behavior).

Teacher 1:
Yes, he/she really has. And I think _____ has also done a really good job of (specific behaviors). I'd like (child already named) to go to the snack table and pass out the napkins and (other child named) to go and pass out the cups.

(Continue dismissing children to the snack table by giving Positive Feedback for their accomplishments and assigning them a task at the snack table. If some children have not earned all of snack, have them practice as follows.)

Teacher 1:
_____, you need to sit here with me and practice (volunteering, keeping hands to self, etc.).

(Ask children questions from the lesson, have them role play, or do relaxation to give them opportunities to practice behaviors that were problematic during relaxation and/or the lesson. As the children practice, watch for a good attitude and effort in practicing and determine when each child seems to have made up for lost opportunities and achieved an acceptable level of competence in the skill or rule following.)

Ask children to clean up snack area.

Teacher 1:
OK, snack time is over now. We need to clean up. _____, would you get the garbage can and bring it around so everyone can throw away the garbage.

(Use Positive Feedback and other Teaching Strategies for cooperating and following directions during the cleanup.)

---

*Activity Time

In addition to today's skill and children's individual target behaviors, give special attention to following group rules, using conversation skills, cooperating, and solving problems.

Explain activity for today's lesson.

Teacher 1:

It's time for an activity now. Today we're going to (describe activity briefly). This is a time for us to practice our target behaviors and Problem Solving.

(Use Activity.)

Ask all the children to help clean up.

Teacher 1:

Now it's time for everyone to help clean up.

(Use Positive Feedback and other Teaching Strategies to help children work well together on cleanup. After cleanup, prompt children to return to circle.)

---

*Home Notes

In addition to today's skill and children's individual target behaviors, give special attention to following group rules and saying nice things.

Divide children into two groups and work on scoring Home Notes.

Teacher 1:

(a child), we are going to talk about how you did during today's session. Who can give (that child) some Positive Feedback and tell him/her good things about how he/she did on (target behavior)?

(Score the top half of the Home Note while the children are giving Positive Feedback. Ask for specific feedback for each of the child's target behaviors and add to it with comments you want to make, pointing out progress and areas needing improvement.)

(same child), now what do you think was the best thing you did in group today?
(child responds or is prompted)

Teacher 1:

That's good.

(Add specific descriptions of strong points.)

You might also try to (suggestions for improvement). Here is your Home Note.

(Repeat sequence with each child.)

---

*New Homework

In addition to today's skill and children's individual target behaviors, give special attention to following group rules and saying nice things.

Pass out Homework.

Teacher 1:

Here is your Homework. Be sure to do it and bring it back next time. Let's see what it says.

(Read aloud.)

If you need help, ask your parents or some other adult in your home.

Role Plays

Situations / Target Behaviors	School Problems (Teacher/Peers)	Neighborhood Problems	Sibling Problems	Parent Problems
Listen Carefully	During reading the teacher calls on you to read out loud, but you don't know where to start.	You're taking care of the neighbors' cat, and you can't remember where they said the key would be.	Your sister asks you to do her a favor and says she'll bring you a treat for doing it. You forgot what she asked you to do.	You are at a friend's, and you aren't sure what time your mom said to be home.
Treat Others Nicely	A kid that everyone calls "nerd" asks you to help her with her math during free time.	A neighbor kid you don't like trips and falls down. One of the lenses in his glasses breaks out and rolls away.	Your sister comes in your room when you are outside and plays with your toys.	You're eating dinner with your family, and you don't like what was cooked.
Join in with Others	At lunch a group of kids are talking about skiing; you'd like to talk to them, but you don't know anything about skiing.	You feel really bored and are riding your bike. You see a group of kids playing basketball. You've never met these kids.	Your mom is taking you and your sister to the movies. They are talking about seeing a movie that is not what you'd choose.	Your aunt is visiting, and she and your family are deciding where to go sightseeing.
Keep a Good Attitude	You get a "C" on your report card, but you think you deserved a better grade.	You are playing ball with a friend, and another kid comes up and takes the ball away from you.	Your little brother hits you, and just as you hit him back, your dad walks in and gets mad at you.	Your dad is watching T.V., and it's almost time for your favorite show.
Take Responsibility for Self	A group of kids are fighting at recess. The teacher is standing close, but you're not sure she will see them.	You and your neighbor are at a movie, and you want some popcorn, but you don't have any money. You still owe this kid money.	Your brother and you are at the store getting some things for your mom. You also want some candy, but there isn't enough money.	You run the vacuum cleaner over a hairpin because you don't think it will matter. Then it makes a loud, awful noise.
Stay Calm and Relaxed	You are on the playground; three kids gang up on you and start calling you a nickname you hate and threatening to hit you.	You are playing softball in front of your house. You hit the ball, and it goes through a neighbor's window. She is very mad.	You have been waiting all day to get home and have a special snack that you bought yesterday. Your sister ate it.	Your mom promised to take you roller-skating, but then tells you she forgot and made plans to get your hair cut.
Solve Problems	You spent your whole allowance over the weekend. On Monday you need some money to buy something at a bake sale at school.	A friend invites you to go to a movie. You agree, but you forgot you already promised to go over to another friend's house.	You're playing a game with your brother, and he keeps moving your "man," taking your turn, etc.	Mom tells you to clean your room before school, and then she leaves. You remember that you have to be at school early today.

Skill 13: Problem Solving
Activity

(The activity provided for Skill 10: Offering to Help can also be used here with Skill 13.)

The materials needed are:

1. Cookies, juice, etc., for snack time.
2. Cups and napkins.
3. Several board games.

This activity should start with snack time. During snack create several "problems" including having too few cups, napkins, cookies, etc. Assign a single child to each task, such as, "Candy, would you get the cups ready for juice?" Watch the child to see if she finds a solution for the problem.

For activity, sabotage three or four board games by removing the spinner, playing pieces, rules, etc. Tell those children who did not problem solve during snack to choose a game and a partner with whom to play. Tell them that they will be in charge of the game.

Give Positive Feedback for spontaneous examples of Problem Solving and use other appropriate Teaching Strategies when necessary to help the children practice Problem Solving.

Skill 13: Problem Solving
Home Note

Name _____ Instructors _____

During today's lesson we practiced problem solving. When faced with a problem (a situation that makes us feel bad or frustrated), we can do things to make the problem either worse or better. To make a problem better and solve it, we practiced staying calm, thinking of at least three different ways to solve our problem, choosing the best way, and trying it first.

Today's Objectives			Target Behaviors	
To solve a problem, did the child:				Score
	YES	NO	A. _____ ___	
			B. _____ ___	
1. Take a deep breath to get a calm body and good attitude?	___	___	C. _____ ___	
			D. _____ ___	
2. Think of at least three different things he/she could do?	___	___	E. _____ ___	
3. Pick the best solution for him/her?	___	___	Score, using this scale: 1 = Completely satisfied 2 = Satisfied	
4. Try that one first?	___	___	3 = Slightly satisfied 4 = Neither satisfied nor dissatisfied 5 = Slightly dissatisfied 6 = Dissatisfied 7 = Completely dissatisfied	

The best thing your child did today in social skills was _____

_____

- -

Parents – Please Complete This Section and Return
Skill 13: Problem Solving

Name _____

The following objectives and target behaviors refer to those named above. Please mark or score your child in these areas and have him/her return this bottom section with your signature to the next social skills group.

Did your child meet the objectives of today's lesson at least once this week?				
	YES	NO	Score your child on his/her target behaviors, using the 1-7 scale above:	
Objective 1	___	___	Target Behavior A _____	
Objective 2	___	___	Target Behavior B _____	
Objective 3	___	___	Target Behavior C _____	
Objective 4	___	___	Target Behavior D _____	
			Target Behavior E _____	

Parent Signature _____ Date _____

Skill 13: Problem Solving
Homework

Name _____

1. Write down a problem you had this week (at home, at school, with someone in your family, or with a friend).

   _____

   _____

   _____

2. Write down three ways to solve the problem.

   a. _____

   _____

   b. _____

   _____

   c. _____

   _____

3. Describe how you solved the problem.

   a. Which way did you choose to best solve your problem? _____

   _____

   b. Why did you choose this way? _____

   _____

4. Explain how a calm body helps in solving problems.

   a. How can you get your body calm when you have a problem?_____

   _____

   b. Why is it important to have a calm body when you have a problem?_____

   _____

Session 14

Skill 14: Using Positive Consequences

YOU MAY SUBSTITUTE naturally occurring events (lunch time, art projects, etc.) for items marked with an asterisk. Be sure to incidentally teach the day's skill, target behaviors, and the behaviors listed whether you use these activities or others. Remember that the dialogue provided in the session outlines (except for the lesson itself) is intended to be a model, not read or memorized verbatim. Read the dialogue over for main points and use your own spontaneous style. **Most of the dialogue and instructions are identical from skill to skill. For efficiency you may wish to attend only to the Relaxation Script number and the new information in the Skill Lesson.**

*Homework Completion and Free Play

In addition to today's skill and children's individual target behaviors, give special attention to taking responsibility, solving problems, and following directions (during Homework completion), and joining in, cooperating, problem solving, keeping a good attitude, and following directions (during free play).

Collect Homework and the bottom half of Home Notes; oversee free play and Homework completion or practice time.

Teacher 1:
(Scan papers to see which children have satisfactorily completed Homework; put aside Home Notes to check later.)

(children who completed it), you may go now and choose a game to play. (children who have not completed it), it's time for you to finish the Homework (or practice the skill) so that you can join the others.

(For children who habitually do not bring completed Homework, add more written questions or role play practice so that they finish about the same time as free play ends.)

Review Homework with children.

Teacher 1:
(Have children form a circle on the floor.)

Now let's look at the Homework you have done. I'm glad that (children who brought completed work) did their work at home. (a child who brought it), will you read your answer to Question _____?

(Have several children who brought their work read answers; ask for feedback from others. If you are using the Homework Progress Chart, allow children to color in the whole square or place a sticker in the square or color in part of it, depending on whether they brought completed Homework or finished it during free play.)

*Relaxation Training

In addition to today's skill and children's individual target behaviors, give special attention to keeping a calm body, solving problems, following directions, and keeping hands to self.

Lead relaxation training.

Teacher 1:
We are going to practice relaxing again. Relaxing will help you learn the new skill and help you face any problem.

(Have children find a place on the floor to lie down. Choose one child to turn off the lights.)

(Use Relaxation Script 6.)

Skill Lesson 14

• Introduce skill and list components.

Teacher 1:
Today we are going to talk about using positive consequences. That means you reward people when they do something you like. That way, they will want to do things you like more often. To use positive consequences, you:
▪ Use a pleasant face and voice.
▪ Do something nice for the person.
For example, you could do the person a favor, thank the person, give the person a hug, or share something.

. . . .

• Role play appropriate example.

Teacher 1:
This is the right way to use positive consequences (reward someone). I'm with my dad, and he has just made me a special snack after school.
Thanks for the snack, dad. Here, I'll help you clean up the dishes.

• Ask children for behavior components of skill.

Teacher 1:
How did you know that was the right way to use positive consequences (reward someone)?
(children respond or are prompted)

• Role play inappropriate example.

Teacher 1:
This is the wrong way to use positive consequences (reward someone). I'm with my dad, and he has just made me a special snack after school.
I'm done with my snack, dad. I'm going outside to play now.

• Ask children for behavior components of skill.

Teacher 1:
What should have happened to make that the right way to use positive consequences (reward someone)?
(children respond or are prompted)

. . . .

• Ask children to role play.

Teacher 1:
Now it is your turn to role play. (Assign role play situation.) I am going to call on someone who has been working really hard in the group by (specific on-task behaviors).
_____ has been working really hard the

whole time by (appropriate behaviors) and looks ready to be the first one to role play. _____, this is your role play.

(Describe the role play you have previously selected for this child from the role play sheet behind this session outline. Have each child role play the skill *correctly* at least one time.)

• Ask children to give Positive Feedback.

Teacher 1 or 2:
Good role playing. Who can give _____ *some Positive Feedback on his/her role play?*

(Call on child who is volunteering and paying attention.)

. . . .

• Ask children for rationales for using skill.

Teacher 1:
Why do you think it is important to use positive consequences with (reward) people when they do things you like?
(children respond or are prompted)

Children:
▪ It will make people want to do those things again.
▪ It will make people feel good.

. . . .

• Lead children through reality check.

Teacher 1:
Sometimes you might try really hard to use positive consequences with (reward) someone when he/she has done something you like, *and this might happen.* I'm with my dad, and he has just made me a special snack after school.
Thanks for the snack, dad. I'll help you clean up the dishes.

Teacher 2:
Well, you'd better help. It's about time you did something to help me out!

Teacher 1:
You just did everything right to use positive consequences with (reward) someone. *What should you do if this happens to you?*
(children respond or are prompted)

Children:
▪ Take a deep breath to get calm.
▪ Keep a good attitude.
▪ Go ahead and do the dishes.
▪ Try again at other times.

*Snack Time

In addition to today's skill and children's individual target behaviors, give special attention to following group rules, using conversation skills, cooperating, and solving problems.

Decide which children have earned all of snack.

Children may earn the entire snack or only a smaller portion if they join the snack in progress. Keep in mind how much difficulty a child has had following rules or practicing during the lesson and relaxation time to get an idea of how much time the child might need to practice to compensate for missed opportunities.

Dismiss children who have already earned snack time to the snack table.

Teacher 1:
OK, it's snack time now. (Teacher 2), who do you think has really been earning snack today?

Teacher 2:
Well, _____ has been really following the rules, having a still body, volunteering, and working on (his/her target behavior).

Teacher 1:
Yes, he/she really has. And I think _____ has also done a really good job of (specific behaviors). I'd like (child already named) to go to the snack table and pass out the napkins and (other child named) to go and pass out the cups.

(Continue dismissing children to the snack table by giving Positive Feedback for their accomplishments and assigning them a task at the snack table. If some children have not earned all of snack, have them practice as follows.)

Teacher 1:
_____, you need to sit here with me and practice (volunteering, keeping hands to self, etc.).

(Ask children questions from the lesson, have them role play, or do relaxation to give them opportunities to practice behaviors that were problematic during relaxation and/or the lesson. As the children practice, watch for a good attitude and effort in practicing and determine when each child seems to have made up for lost opportunities and achieved an acceptable level of competence in the skill or rule following.)

Ask children to clean up snack area.

Teacher 1:
OK, snack time is over now. We need to clean up. _____, would you get the garbage can and bring it around so everyone can throw away the garbage.

(Use Positive Feedback and other Teaching Strategies for cooperating and following directions during the cleanup.)

---

*Activity Time

In addition to today's skill and children's individual target behaviors, give special attention to following group rules, using conversation skills, cooperating, and solving problems.

Explain activity for today's lesson.

Teacher 1:
It's time for an activity now. Today we're going to (describe activity briefly). This is a time for us to practice our target behaviors and Using Positive Consequences (rewarding someone).

(Use Activity.)

Ask all the children to help clean up.

Teacher 1:
Now it's time for everyone to help clean up.

(Use Positive Feedback and other Teaching Strategies to help children work well together on cleanup. After cleanup, prompt children to return to circle.)

---

*Home Notes

In addition to today's skill and children's individual target behaviors, give special attention to following group rules and saying nice things.

Divide children into two groups and work on scoring Home Notes.

Teacher 1:
(a child), we are going to talk about how you did during today's session. Who can give (that child) some Positive Feedback and tell him/her good things about how he/she did on (target behavior)?

(Score the top half of the Home Note while the children are giving Positive Feedback. Ask for specific feedback for each of the child's target behaviors and add to it with comments you want to make, pointing out progress and areas needing improvement.)

(same child), now what do you think was the best thing you did in group today?
(child responds or is prompted)

Teacher 1:
That's good.

(Add specific descriptions of strong points.)

You might also try to (suggestions for improvement). Here is your Home Note.

(Repeat sequence with each child.)

---

*New Homework

In addition to today's skill and children's individual target behaviors, give special attention to following group rules and saying nice things.

Pass out Homework.

Teacher 1:
Here is your Homework. Be sure to do it and bring it back next time. Let's see what it says.

(Read aloud.)

If you need help, ask your parents or some other adult in your home.

Relaxation Script 6

(This script may be used in conjunction with Skill 14. Please review the section on relaxation training in Chapter 5 of the Guide.)

Today we will be practicing how to relax while sitting up with the lights on. That way we can relax while we are at school and home. First, sit with your legs crossed, your back straight yet relaxed, and your arms lying loosely in your lap.

Now as I count to three, breathe in slowly, and as you breathe out, think the words "I AM CALM." (count aloud slowly) One . . . two . . . three. (pause) Relax. Now your body is ready to relax.

Think about your face. If there is any tightness in your forehead, mouth, or eyes, let them go smooth. (pause) As I count to three, breathe in slowly, and as you breathe out, think the words "I AM CALM." (count aloud slowly) One . . . two . . . three. (pause) Relax.

Think about your shoulders. If they are feeling tight, let them go soft and loose. (pause) As I count to three, breathe in slowly, and as you breathe out, think the words "I AM CALM." (count aloud slowly) One . . . two . . . three. (pause) Relax.

Now think about your arms and hands. If they are feeling tight, let them relax loosely in your lap. (pause) As I count to three, breathe in slowly, and as you breathe out, think the words "I AM CALM." (count aloud slowly) One . . . two . . . three. (pause) Relax.

Think about your stomach and back. If they are feeling upset or tight, let them go soft and loose. As I count to three, breathe in slowly, and as you breathe out, think the words "I AM CALM." (count aloud slowly) One . . . two . . . three. (pause) Relax.

Now think about your legs and feet. If they are feeling tight or wiggly, let them relax. Your legs feel calm and loose. (pause) As I count to three, breathe in slowly, and as you breathe out, think the words "I AM CALM." (count aloud slowly) One . . . two . . . three. (pause) Relax.

Now that your body is relaxed, I want you to imagine that your new bike has a flat tire. Your older brother is raking the lawn, but he offers to loan you his bike. Your body is feeling so tense, your stomach and face muscles so tight, that you almost forget to thank your brother or offer to help him rake the lawn. (pause) If any parts of your body are feeling tense, let them relax. They should feel soft and loose. (pause) As I count to three, breathe in slowly, and as you breathe out, think the words "I AM CALM." (count aloud slowly) One . . . two . . . three. (pause) Relax. One more time, keep your body loose and relaxed and imagine yourself with a problem that your brother helps you solve. (pause) As I count to three, breathe in slowly, and as you breathe out, think the words "I AM CALM." (count aloud slowly) One . . . two . . . three. (pause) Relax. Now your body feels calm and relaxed and you can remember to thank your brother.

Now I want you to think of the last time you had a problem with someone. (pause and give children a chance to think of their own situations) Imagine yourself with this problem. (pause) Think about how your body feels. Your stomach gets a knot in it, and your face and arms feel tense. (pause) If your body feels tense, let it relax; make your muscles soft and loose. (pause) As I count to three, breathe in slowly, and as you breathe out, think the words "I AM CALM." (count aloud slowly) One . . . two . . . three. (pause) Relax. One more time, keep your body loose and relaxed and imagine yourself having this problem. (pause) As I count to three, breathe in slowly, and as you breathe out, think the words "I AM CALM." (count aloud slowly) One . . . two . . . three. (pause) Relax.

Now your body feels calm and relaxed. The next time you have a problem and begin to feel upset, sad, or angry, remember to take a slow deep breath and relax your body; then you will be able to solve your problem and remember to thank those who help you.

Skill 14: Using Positive Consequences
Role Plays

Situations / Target Behaviors	School Problems (Teacher/Peers)	Neighborhood Problems	Sibling Problems	Parent Problems
Listen Carefully	You did great on your math test; your teacher gives you lots of choices for free time. You see your teacher begin to clean the art table.	Your friend invites you to go swimming at her house. She then gives you the details about how to get there.	After your sister agrees to let you wear her pretty blouse, she tells you that she likes some of your new clothes and toys.	Dad offers to take you out to lunch for pizza. He then tells you all of the different chores he has to do in the yard today.
Treat Others Nicely	A kid in school who is called names brings a neat new toy to school and offers to let you play with it.	There's a kid on the block who usually won't play with you. Today he is really friendly and asks you to play.	Your sister offers to help you finish your chores so you can go to the movies. You're leaving in half an hour.	You're going away to camp. Mom has just washed all the laundry so that you'll have plenty of clean clothes.
Join in with Others	Your friend has brownies for dessert and asks if you want one. You have grapes in your lunch.	Some kids playing near your house ask you to join them. You can't; your mother just called you in for lunch.	Your brother (or sister) who usually makes all the decisions about what to play asks you what *you* want to play.	Your mom and dad are in the middle of a game you like. They invite you to join them.
Keep a Good Attitude	A kid who sits with you on the school bus usually asks you to open your lunch and share your dessert. Today he doesn't.	Your friend offers to let you try out his new bicycle. You just got a skateboard for your birthday.	You've been wanting to get this special game for a long time. Your sister gives it to you for your birthday.	Dad gets home early today and asks if you would like to go on a bicycle ride.
Take Responsibility for Self	You lose your lunch money. When you tell the teacher, she offers to loan you money for lunch. She's tidying the classroom.	You borrow a friend's kite and get it tangled in a tree. You tell her what happened, and she offers to help untangle it.	Your brother is treating you to a movie. Before you sit down, you both decide to buy popcorn.	You come home early from school and see that your mom has cleaned your bedroom for you.
Stay Calm and Relaxed	A big kid on the playground, who usually bullies you, is nice to you and invites you to play basketball.	You're playing checkers with a friend who *always* wants to go first. This time your friend offers to let you go first.	You're watching T.V. with your sister, and she asks you which show you want to watch next. Usually she never lets you choose.	Your dad helped you with your homework. Now he has to finish cleaning the family room. Your favorite T.V. program is just starting.
Solve Problems	Your friend usually borrows a pencil or eraser from your desk without asking. This time your friend asks.	Your friend invites you to spend the night. You would like to, but your family is going away for the weekend.	Your bike has a flat tire. You ask to borrow your brother's bike, and he agrees. He is doing yard work.	On a snowy day you ask mom to drive you around to deliver your newspapers. She's doing the dishes, but says, "Yes."

Skill 14: Using Positive Consequences
Activity

(The activity provided for Skill 9: Sharing can also be used here with Skill 14.)

The materials needed are:

1. Junk (for junk sculptures).
2. Prizes (one pack of gum and two cookies for each pair of children).
3. Heavy paper or cardboard.
4. Paste.

Divide the children into pairs; give one of the pair the gum and the other the cookies. Give an assortment of junk and paper to each pair. Each child will work on his/her own junk sculpture to take home. The children will have to negotiate for items of junk; this should provide opportunities for Sharing, Compromising, and Using Positive Consequences. Children may even want to share some of their snack to show their appreciation of one another's sharing, etc.

Use Positive Feedback when the children correctly use the target skills.

Skill 14: Using Positive Consequences
Home Note

Name _____ Instructors _____

During today's lesson we practiced using positive consequences with (rewarding) a person when he/she does something we like. This way, the person may want to do things to please us more often.

Today's Objectives	Target Behaviors

Today's Objectives

To use positive consequences – reward someone – did the child:

	YES	NO
1. Use a pleasant face and voice?	_____	_____
2. Do something nice for the person?	_____	_____

For example, the child could have done the person a favor, thanked the person, given the person a hug, or shared something.

Target Behaviors

		Score
A.	_____	_____
B.	_____	_____
C.	_____	_____
D.	_____	_____
E.	_____	_____

Score, using this scale:
1 = Completely satisfied
2 = Satisfied
3 = Slightly satisfied
4 = Neither satisfied nor dissatisfied
5 = Slightly dissatisfied
6 = Dissatisfied
7 = Completely dissatisfied

The best thing your child did today in social skills was _____
_____

- -

Parents – Please Complete This Section and Return
Skill 14: Using Positive Consequences

Name _____

The following objectives and target behaviors refer to those named above. Please mark or score your child in these areas and have him/her return this bottom section with your signature to the next social skills group.

Did your child meet the objectives of today's lesson at least once this week?

	YES	NO
Objective 1	_____	_____
Objective 2	_____	_____

Score your child on his/her target behaviors, using the 1-7 scale above:

Target Behavior A _____

Target Behavior B _____

Target Behavior C _____

Target Behavior D _____

Target Behavior E _____

Parent Signature _____ Date _____

Skill 14: Using Positive Consequences
Homework

Name _____

1. Write down four different ways you can use positive consequences – reward someone – when the person does something you like.

   a. _____
   _____

   b. _____
   _____

   c. _____
   _____

   d. _____
   _____

2. Try rewarding your mom, dad, brother, or sister each time she/he does something nice. Name two times when you rewarded someone in your family.

   Time 1:

   a. Who did you reward? _____
   _____

   b. What did you do or say? _____
   _____

   c. What did the other person do or say? _____
   _____

   Time 2:

   a. Who did you reward? _____
   _____

   b. What did you do or say? _____
   _____

   c. What did the other person do or say? _____
   _____

3. Reward a friend for doing something nice.

   a. What did you reward for? _____
   _____

   b. What did you do or say? _____
   _____

Session 15

Skill 15: Giving and Receiving a Suggestion for Improvement

YOU MAY SUBSTITUTE naturally occurring events (lunch time, art projects, etc.) for items marked with an asterisk. Be sure to incidentally teach the day's skill, target behaviors, and the behaviors listed whether you use these activities or others. Remember that the dialogue provided in the session outlines (except for the lesson itself) is intended to be a model, not read or memorized verbatim. Read the dialogue over for main points and use your own spontaneous style. **Most of the dialogue and instructions are identical from skill to skill. For efficiency you may wish to attend only to the Relaxation Script number and the new information in the Skill Lesson.**

---

*Homework Completion and Free Play

In addition to today's skill and children's individual target behaviors, give special attention to taking responsibility, solving problems, and following directions (during Homework completion), and joining in, cooperating, problem solving, keeping a good attitude, and following directions (during free play).

Collect Homework and the bottom half of Home Notes; oversee free play and Homework completion or practice time.

Teacher 1:
(Scan papers to see which children have satisfactorily completed Homework; put aside Home Notes to check later.)

(children who completed it), you may go now and choose a game to play. (children who have not completed it), it's time for you to finish the Homework (or practice the skill) so that you can join the others.

(For children who habitually do not bring completed Homework, add more written questions or role play practice so that they finish about the same time as free play ends.)

Review Homework with children.

Teacher 1:
(Have children form a circle on the floor.)

Now let's look at the Homework you have done. I'm glad that (children who brought completed work) did their work at home. (a child who brought it), will you read your answer to Question _____?

(Have several children who brought their work read answers; ask for feedback from others. If you are using the Homework Progress Chart, allow children to color in the whole square or place a sticker in the square or color in part of it, depending on whether they brought completed Homework or finished it during free play.)

---

*Relaxation Training

In addition to today's skill and children's individual target behaviors, give special attention to keeping a calm body, solving problems, following directions, and keeping hands to self.

Lead relaxation training.

Teacher 1:
We are going to practice relaxing again. Relaxing will help you learn the new skill and help you face any problem.

(Have children find a place on the floor to lie down. Choose one child to turn off the lights.)

(Use Relaxation Script 7.)

Skill Lesson 15

● **Introduce skill and list components.**

Teacher 1:
Today we are going to talk about giving and receiving a suggestion for improvement. When you and another person have a problem getting along, the two of you can work on the problem together by giving and receiving suggestions for improving the situation. To give a suggestion for improvement, you:
▪ Use a pleasant face and voice.
▪ Say something nice on the topic ("I like the way you. . .").
▪ Make the suggestion ("It would be better if. . .").
▪ Thank the person for listening ("Thanks for listening").
To receive a suggestion for improvement, you:
▪ Use a pleasant face and voice.
▪ Listen to the suggestion.
▪ Make no excuses.
▪ Thank the person for the suggestion ("Thanks for the suggestion").

. . . .

● **Role play appropriate example.**

Teacher 1:
This is the right way to give and receive a suggestion for improvement. I ask my friend to play. She wants to decide which game to play.
I really like playing with you; it would be nice if you would let me decide what to play sometimes.

Teacher 2:
I didn't know that you feel that way. Thanks for telling me that.

Teacher 1:
Thanks for listening.

● **Ask children for behavior components of skill.**

Teacher 1:
How did you know that was the right way to give and receive a suggestion for improvement?
(children respond or are prompted)

● **Role play inappropriate example.**

Teacher 1:
This is the wrong way to give and receive a suggestion for improvement. I ask my friend to play. She wants to decide which game to play.
You're no fun to play with at all! You always do all the good stuff, like deciding what to play!

Teacher 2:
Well, if I didn't decide, you wouldn't have any good ideas about what to play!

● **Ask children for behavior components of skill.**

Teacher 1:
What should have happened to make that the right way to give and receive a suggestion for improvement? (children respond or are prompted)

. . . .

● **Ask children to role play.**

Teacher 1:
Now it is your turn to role play. (Assign role play situation.) I am going to call on someone who has been working really hard in the group by (specific on-task behaviors).
_____ has been working really hard the whole time by (appropriate behaviors) and looks ready to be the first one to role play. _____, this is your role play.

(Describe the role play you have previously selected for this child from the role play sheet behind this session outline. Have each child role play the skill *correctly* at least one time.)

● **Ask children to give Positive Feedback.**

Teacher 1 or 2:
Good role playing. Who can give _____ *some Positive Feedback on his/her role play?*

(Call on child who is volunteering and paying attention.)

. . . .

● **Ask children for rationales for using skill.**

Teacher 1:
Why do you think it is important to give and receive suggestions for improvement?
(children respond or are prompted)

Children:
▪ It helps you to solve problems without making people feel bad.
▪ You feel better when you get along with other people.

. . . .

● **Lead children through reality check.**

Teacher 1:
Sometimes you might try really hard to give or receive a suggestion for improvement, *and this might happen.* I ask my friend to play. She wants to decide which game to play.

132

I really like playing with you; it would be nice if you would let me decide what to play sometimes.

Teacher 2:
What a dumb idea! I don't want to play with you at all!

Teacher 1:
You just did everything right to give a suggestion for improvement. *What should you do if this happens to you?* (children respond or are prompted)

Children:
- Take a deep breath to get calm.
- Keep a good attitude.
- Try it again later.
- Find someone else to play with.
- Realize that some people just don't know how to receive (or give) a suggestion for improvement.

*Snack Time

In addition to today's skill and children's individual target behaviors, give special attention to following group rules, using conversation skills, cooperating, and solving problems.

Decide which children have earned all of snack.

Children may earn the entire snack or only a smaller portion if they join the snack in progress. Keep in mind how much difficulty a child has had following rules or practicing during the lesson and relaxation time to get an idea of how much time the child might need to practice to compensate for missed opportunities.

Dismiss children who have already earned snack time to the snack table.

Teacher 1:
OK, it's snack time now. (Teacher 2), who do you think has really been earning snack today?

Teacher 2:
Well, _____ has been really following the rules, having a still body, volunteering, and working on (his/her target behavior).

Teacher 1:
Yes, he/she really has. And I think _____ has also done a really good job of (specific behaviors). I'd like (child already named) to go to the snack table and pass out the napkins and (other child named) to go and pass out the cups.

(Continue dismissing children to the snack table by giving Positive Feedback for their accomplishments and assigning them a task at the snack table. If some children have not earned all of snack, have them practice as follows.)

Teacher 1:
_____, you need to sit here with me and practice (volunteering, keeping hands to self, etc.).

(Ask children questions from the lesson, have them role play, or do relaxation to give them opportunities to practice behaviors that were problematic during relaxation and/or the lesson. As the children practice, watch for a good attitude and effort in practicing and determine when each child seems to have made up for lost opportunities and achieved an acceptable level of competence in the skill or rule following.)

Ask children to clean up snack area.

Teacher 1:
OK, snack time is over now. We need to clean up. _____, would you get the garbage can and bring it around so everyone can throw away the garbage.

(Use Positive Feedback and other Teaching Strategies for cooperating and following directions during the cleanup.)

*Activity Time

In addition to today's skill and children's individual target behaviors, give special attention to following group rules, using conversation skills, cooperating, and solving problems.

Explain activity for today's lesson.

Teacher 1:
It's time for an activity now. Today we're going to (describe activity briefly). This is a time for us to practice our target behaviors and Giving and Receiving a Suggestion for Improvement.

(Use Activity.)

Ask all the children to help clean up.

Teacher 1:
Now it's time for everyone to help clean up.

(Use Positive Feedback and other Teaching Strategies to help children work well together on cleanup. After cleanup, prompt children to return to circle.)

---

*Home Notes

In addition to today's skill and children's individual target behaviors, give special attention to following group rules and saying nice things.

Divide children into two groups and work on scoring Home Notes.

Teacher 1:
(a child), we are going to talk about how you did during today's session. Who can give (that child) some Positive Feedback and tell him/her good things about how he/she did on (target behavior)?

(Score the top half of the Home Note while the children are giving Positive Feedback. Ask for specific feedback for each of the child's target behaviors and add to it with comments you want to make, pointing out progress and areas needing improvement.)

(same child), now what do you think was the best thing you did in group today?
(child responds or is prompted)

Teacher 1:
That's good.

(Add specific descriptions of strong points.)

You might also try to (suggestions for improvement). Here is your Home Note.

(Repeat sequence with each child.)

---

*New Homework

In addition to today's skill and children's individual target behaviors, give special attention to following group rules and saying nice things.

Pass out Homework.

Teacher 1:
Here is your Homework. Be sure to do it and bring it back next time. Let's see what it says.

(Read aloud.)

If you need help, ask your parents or some other adult in your home.

Relaxation Script 7

(This script may be used in conjunction with Skills 15 and 16. Please review the section on relaxation training in Chapter 5 of the Guide.)

Today we'll be learning how to relax while sitting in a chair; that way we will be able to relax without others noticing. We can even relax at our desks at school or while sitting at the dinner table at home. (pause) First, I want you to sit with your bottom flat in the chair and your feet touching the floor. (pause) Your back should be resting comfortably against the back of the chair, your face looking forward, and your eyes closed. Your arms are lying loosely in your lap. (pause) As I count to three, breathe in slowly, and as you breathe out, think the words "I AM CALM." (count aloud slowly) One . . . two . . . three. (pause) Relax. Now your body is ready to relax.

Think about your face. If there is any tightness in your forehead, mouth, or eyes, let them go smooth. (pause) As I count to three, breathe in slowly, and as you breathe out, think the words "I AM CALM." (count aloud slowly) One . . . two . . . three. (pause) Relax.

Think about your shoulders. If they are feeling tight, let them go soft and loose. (pause) As I count to three, breathe in slowly, and as you breathe out, think the words "I AM CALM." (count aloud slowly) One . . . two . . . three. (pause) Relax.

Now think about your arms and hands. If they are feeling tight, let them relax loosely in your lap. (pause) As I count to three, breathe in slowly, and as you breathe out, think the words "I AM CALM." (count aloud slowly) One . . . two . . . three. (pause) Relax.

Think about your stomach and back. If they are feeling upset or tight, let them go soft and loose. (pause) As I count to three, breathe in slowly, and as you breathe out, think the words "I AM CALM." (count aloud slowly) One . . . two . . . three. (pause) Relax.

Now think about your legs and feet. If they are feeling tight or wiggly, let them relax. Your legs feel calm and loose. (pause) As I count to three, breathe in slowly, and as you breathe out, think the words "I AM CALM." (count aloud slowly) One . . . two . . . three. (pause) Relax.

Now that your body is relaxed, I want you to imagine that you're having a problem with your sister or brother. She/he always borrows your toys but never remembers to put them away afterwards. You walk in your room, and your games are scattered everywhere. Your body feels angry. Think about how your body feels; your arms, stomach, and face may feel tense. (pause) If any parts of your body feel tense, let them relax. (pause) As I count to three, breathe in slowly, and as you breathe out, think the words "I AM CALM." (count aloud slowly) One . . . two . . . three. (pause) Relax. One more time, keep your body loose and relaxed and imagine yourself walking into your messy room. (pause) As I count to three, breathe in slowly, and as you breathe out, think the words "I AM CALM." (count aloud slowly) One . . . two . . . three. (pause) Relax. Now you can keep calm and tell your brother or sister about the problem without getting upset.

Now I want you to imagine yourself out on the playground. The kids are picking teams for a kickball game. One captain chooses you, another kid on the team moans and says things like, "Not him, he's the worst player, he can't even run fast, how do you expect him to kick?" Your body feels angry, and your feelings are hurt. Think about how your body feels; your stomach and arms tighten; you feel yourself wanting to cry or say mean things back to that person. (pause) If any parts of your body are feeling tense, let them relax. (pause) As I count to three, breathe in slowly, and as you breathe out, think the words "I AM CALM." (count aloud slowly) One . . . two . . . three. (pause) Relax. One more time, keep your body loose and relaxed and think of someone giving you a hard time and calling you names. (pause) As I count to three, breathe in slowly, and as you breathe out, think the words "I AM CALM." (count aloud slowly) One . . . two . . . three. (pause) Relax. Now you can play a game, keep calm, and have fun with the kids who are playing nicely.

Now your body feels calm and relaxed. The next time you find yourself having a problem with someone else and your body feels upset, hurt, or angry, remember to take a slow deep breath and relax your body. When your body is calm, it is easier to take care of the problems you have with other people.

Skill 15: Giving and Receiving a Suggestion for Improvement
Role Plays

Situations Target Behaviors	School Problems (Teacher/Peers)	Neighborhood Problems	Sibling Problems	Parent Problems
Listen Carefully	Two kids behind you keep talking during class, and you can't hear the teacher.	You are talking to a friend, and his little brother keeps trying to show you a new toy.	Your sister asks you to do something for her as she is going out the door and not facing you.	Your mom is telling you your chores for the day but keeps getting distracted by watching the news on T.V.
Treat Others Nicely	The nurse at the school keeps getting you confused with another kid who looks a little bit like you.	A neighbor kid keeps following you around and asking to play with you. You have other friends you'd rather play with.	You and your friend are talking; your little brother comes up and interrupts.	Your mom keeps cooking something you don't like because it's fast. You would help more if you could have what you want.
Join in with Others	You bring your new ball to school. Your friends want to play kickball, but you want to play basketball.	You have a friend you like to play with a lot, but she never lets you choose what to play.	You really like to play with your sister, but she never lets you go first.	Your parents and older sister are deciding what movie the family should see tonight. You know what you'd like to see.
Keep a Good Attitude	You are playing ball on the playground, and a kid comes by and kicks the ball away from you.	Your friend is always asking to borrow your bike, but he keeps leaving it out where it might get stolen.	Your brother just came over and changed the T.V. channel while you were watching a show you like.	Your dad cleaned out your room and threw away some things you wanted to keep.
Take Responsibility for Self	At recess a friend offers to pass you the answers during the math test you're afraid of failing.	A friend is at your house playing with you. He always leaves without helping put toys away. It is time for him to go.	Your brother tells you he will do your homework for you. Your mom said you both could go skating when it was done.	Your dad returned your library books for you without asking. You had to renew them for a project you were doing.
Stay Calm and Relaxed	The kid behind you in class keeps kicking her foot against your chair, and you can't write your answers to the test.	You are playing basketball with your friend, but he keeps hogging the ball.	Your little sister was in your room playing your records, and one got scratched.	Your mom is yelling at you again – this time about putting your clothes in the right laundry basket.
Solve Problems	You are assigned to work on a project with some other kids. You feel like you are doing all the work.	Your neighbor walks her dog by your house, and it walks through the flower bed you take care of.	You and your sister got a new game for Christmas. She wants to play it with you, but you're afraid you will have to clean up.	Your mom keeps picking you up late, and you don't like hanging around school so late.

Skill 15: Giving and Receiving a Suggestion for Improvement
Activity

The materials needed are:

1. Paper.
2. Crayons, markers, pencils, etc., for drawing or painting pictures.

Pair the children. Give each child a piece of paper and box of crayons or set of markers. One child will describe to his/her partner a picture or scene, and the partner will attempt to draw a picture of the scene described. That child will give suggestions to his/her partner for improving the picture to make it more like what he/she had imagined (e.g., "That's exactly the right color for that tree. It would be nice if it were taller"). Children then switch roles.

This is a difficult skill for children (as well as adults!). Therefore, before the children make their suggestions, you will need to model several appropriate examples of suggestions for improvement. Some coaching may also be needed, particularly to help the children with the first component of the skill (i.e., saying something nice about the picture). Use Positive Feedback when children correctly give and receive suggestions for improvement.

Skill 15: Giving and Receiving a Suggestion for Improvement
Home Note

Name _____ Instructors _____

During today's lesson we practiced giving and receiving constructive criticism. When we are having trouble getting along with another person, we can give that person a suggestion for change or improvement, or that person may give us a suggestion for change or improvement.

Today's Objectives			Target Behaviors	
To give a suggestion for improvement, did the child:*				Score
	YES	NO	A. _____	_____
1. Use a pleasant face and voice?	_____	_____	B. _____	_____
2. Say something nice on the topic?	_____	_____	C. _____	_____
3. Make the suggestion?	_____	_____	D. _____	_____
4. Thank the person for listening?	_____	_____	E. _____	_____

To receive a suggestion for improvement, did the child:

5. Use a pleasant face and voice? _____ _____
6. Listen to the suggestion? _____ _____
7. Make no excuses? _____ _____
8. Thank the person for the suggestion? _____ _____

Score, using this scale:
1 = Completely satisfied
2 = Satisfied
3 = Slightly satisfied
4 = Neither satisfied nor dissatisfied
5 = Slightly dissatisfied
6 = Dissatisfied
7 = Completely dissatisfied

The best thing your child did today in social skills was _____
_____

- -

Parents – Please Complete This Section and Return
Skill 15: Giving and Receiving a Suggestion for Improvement

Name _____

The following objectives and target behaviors refer to those named above. Please mark or score your child in these areas and have him/her return this bottom section with your signature to the next social skills group.

Did your child meet the objectives of today's lesson at least once this week?

	YES	NO
Objective 1	_____	_____
Objective 2	_____	_____
Objective 3	_____	_____
Objective 4	_____	_____
Objective 5	_____	_____
Objective 6	_____	_____
Objective 7	_____	_____
Objective 8	_____	_____

Score your child on his/her target behaviors, using the 1-7 scale above:

Target Behavior A _____
Target Behavior B _____
Target Behavior C _____
Target Behavior D _____
Target Behavior E _____

Parent Signature _____ Date _____

*Suggested dialogue for young or low-functioning children is "I like the way you . . . ," "It would be better if . . . ," and "Thanks for listening."

138

Skill 15: Giving and Receiving a Suggestion for Improvement
Homework

Name _____

1. What are three things you should do when giving someone a suggestion on how to improve?

    a. _____
    _____

    b. _____
    _____

    c. _____
    _____

2. Tell about a problem you had with someone at home or school this week.

    a. What was the problem? _____
    _____

    b. What was something nice that you said?_____
    _____

    c. What was the suggestion for improvement that you gave?_____
    _____

    d. What did the other person do or say?_____
    _____

3. When you give someone a suggestion on how to improve, why is it important to first say something nice?

    _____
    _____

4. Tell about a time this week your mom, dad, teacher, or some other adult gave you a suggestion for improvement.

    a. What was the person's suggestion for improvement?_____
    _____

    b. What did you do or say? _____
    _____

Session 16

Skill 16: Handling Name-Calling and Teasing

YOU MAY SUBSTITUTE naturally occurring events (lunch time, art projects, etc.) for items marked with an asterisk. Be sure to incidentally teach the day's skill, target behaviors, and the behaviors listed whether you use these activities or others. Remember that the dialogue provided in the session outlines (except for the lesson itself) is intended to be a model, not read or memorized verbatim. Read the dialogue over for main points and use your own spontaneous style. **Most of the dialogue and instructions are identical from skill to skill. For efficiency you may wish to attend only to the Relaxation Script number and the new information in the Skill Lesson.**

---

*Homework Completion and Free Play

In addition to today's skill and children's individual target behaviors, give special attention to taking responsibility, solving problems, and following directions (during Homework completion), and joining in, cooperating, problem solving, keeping a good attitude, and following directions (during free play).

Collect Homework and the bottom half of Home Notes; oversee free play and Homework completion or practice time.

Teacher 1:
(Scan papers to see which children have satisfactorily completed Homework; put aside Home Notes to check later.)

(children who completed it), you may go now and choose a game to play. (children who have not completed it), it's time for you to finish the Homework (or practice the skill) so that you can join the others.

(For children who habitually do not bring completed Homework, add more written questions or role play practice so that they finish about the same time as free play ends.)

Review Homework with children.

Teacher 1:
(Have children form a circle on the floor.)

Now let's look at the Homework you have done. I'm glad that (children who brought completed work) did their work at home. (a child who brought it), will you read your answer to Question _____?

(Have several children who brought their work read answers; ask for feedback from others. If you are using the Homework Progress Chart, allow children to color in the whole square or place a sticker in the square or color in part of it, depending on whether they brought completed Homework or finished it during free play.)

---

*Relaxation Training

In addition to today's skill and children's individual target behaviors, give special attention to keeping a calm body, solving problems, following directions, and keeping hands to self.

Lead relaxation training.

Teacher 1:
We are going to practice relaxing again. Relaxing will help you learn the new skill and help you face any problem.

(Have children find a place on the floor to lie down. Choose one child to turn off the lights.)

(Use Relaxation Script 7.)

Skill Lesson 16

• Introduce skill and list components.

Teacher 1:
Today we are going to talk about handling name-calling and teasing. To handle name-calling and teasing, you:
- Keep a pleasant face.
- Take a deep breath to get calm.
- Look away or walk away if you can.
- Use positive self-talk.

Positive self-talk is something you say to yourself that makes you feel good; for example, "I'm calm. I can handle this. I can ignore."

. . . .

• Role play appropriate example.

Teacher 1:
This is the right way to handle name-calling and teasing. I'm on the playground, and another kid is calling me names.

Teacher 2:
You're stupid and ugly and no fun to play with, and I hate you!

Teacher 1:
(takes a deep breath, stays calm, looks away, maintains a pleasant face) I'm thinking, "I'm OK; I can keep calm; I don't need to get mad."

• Ask children for behavior components of skill.

Teacher 1:
How did you know that was the right way to handle name-calling and teasing?
(children respond or are prompted)

• Role play inappropriate example.

Teacher 1:
This is the wrong way to handle name-calling and teasing. I'm on the playground, and another kid is calling me names.

Teacher 2:
You're stupid and ugly and no fun to play with, and I hate you!

Teacher 1:
(fidgets, gives eye contact, develops angry expression) Well, I don't care what you think anyway, you creep!

• Ask children for behavior components of skill.

Teacher 1:
What should have happened to make that the right way to handle name-calling and teasing?

(children respond or are prompted)

. . . .

• Ask children to role play.

Teacher 1:
Now it is your turn to role play. (Assign role play situation.) I am going to call on someone who has been working really hard in the group by (specific on-task behaviors). _____ has been working really hard the whole time by (appropriate behaviors) and looks ready to be the first one to role play. _____, this is your role play.

(Describe the role play you have previously selected for this child from the role play sheet behind this session outline. Have each child role play the skill *correctly* at least one time.)

• Ask children to give Positive Feedback.

Teacher 1 or 2:
Good role playing. Who can give _____ *some Positive Feedback on his/her role play?*

(Call on child who is volunteering and paying attention.)

. . . .

• Ask children for rationales for using skill.

Teacher 1:
Why do you think it is important to handle name-calling and teasing?
(children respond or are prompted)

Children:
- You can feel better about yourself.
- Others will tease you less.
- You can avoid getting in trouble.

. . . .

• Lead children through reality check.

Teacher 1:
Sometimes you might try really hard to handle name-calling and teasing, *and this might happen.* I'm on the playground, and another kid is calling me names.

Teacher 2:
You're stupid and ugly and no fun to play with, and I hate you!

Teacher 1:
(takes a deep breath, stays calm, looks away, maintains pleasant face) I'm thinking, "I'm all right; I'm calm; I don't need to get mad."

Teacher 2:
I wish you'd get lost! You nerd. (heckling continues)

Teacher 1:
You just did everything right to handle name-calling and teasing. *What should you do if this happens to you?* (children respond or are prompted)

Children:
- Take a deep breath to get calm.
- Keep a good attitude.
- Keep ignoring.
- Walk away from that person.
- Talk to someone else.

---

*Snack Time

In addition to today's skill and children's individual target behaviors, give special attention to following group rules, using conversation skills, cooperating, and solving problems. Also use additional activity (party planning) during snack time.

Decide which children have earned all of snack.

Children may earn the entire snack or only a smaller portion if they join the snack in progress. Keep in mind how much difficulty a child has had following rules or practicing during the lesson and relaxation time to get an idea of how much time the child might need to practice to compensate for missed opportunities.

Dismiss children who have already earned snack time to the snack table.

Teacher 1:
OK, it's snack time now. (Teacher 2), who do you think has really been earning snack today?

Teacher 2:
Well, _____ has been really following the rules, having a still body, volunteering, and working on (his/her target behavior).

Teacher 1:
Yes, he/she really has. And I think _____ has also done a really good job of (specific behaviors). I'd like (child already named) to go to the snack table and pass out the napkins and (other child named) to go and pass out the cups.

(Continue dismissing children to the snack table by giving Positive Feedback for their accomplishments and assigning them a task at the snack table. If some children have not earned all of snack, have them practice as follows.)

Teacher 1:
_____, you need to sit here with me and practice (volunteering, keeping hands to self, etc.).

(Ask children questions from the lesson, have them role play, or do relaxation to give them opportunities to practice behaviors that were problematic during relaxation and/or the lesson. As the children practice, watch for a good attitude and effort in practicing and determine when each child seems to have made up for lost opportunities and achieved an acceptable level of competence in the skill or rule following.)

Ask children to clean up snack area.

Teacher 1:
OK, snack time is over now. We need to clean up. _____, would you get the garbage can and bring it around so everyone can throw away the garbage.

(Use Positive Feedback and other Teaching Strategies for cooperating and following directions during the cleanup.)

---

*Activity Time

In addition to today's skill and children's individual target behaviors, give special attention to following group rules, using conversation skills, cooperating, and solving problems.

Explain activity for today's lesson.

Teacher 1:
It's time for an activity now. Today we're going to (describe activity briefly). This is a time for us to practice our target behaviors and Handling Name-Calling and Teasing.

(Use Activity.)

Ask all the children to help clean up.

Teacher 1:
Now it's time for everyone to help clean up.

(Use Positive Feedback and other Teaching Strategies to help children work well together on cleanup. After cleanup, prompt children to return to circle.)

---

*Home Notes

In addition to today's skill and children's individual target behaviors, give special attention to following group rules and saying nice things.

Divide children into two groups and work on scoring Home Notes.

Teacher 1:
(a child), we are going to talk about how you did during today's session. Who can give (that child) some Positive Feedback and tell him/her good things about how he/she did on (target behavior)?

(Score the top half of the Home Note while the children are giving Positive Feedback. Ask for specific feedback for each of the child's target behaviors and add to it with comments you want to make, pointing out progress and areas needing improvement.)

(same child), now what do you think was the best thing you did in group today?
(child responds or is prompted)

Teacher 1:
That's good.

(Add specific descriptions of strong points.)

You might also try to (suggestions for improvement). Here is your Home Note.

(Repeat sequence with each child.)

---

*New Homework

In addition to today's skill and children's individual target behaviors, give special attention to following group rules and saying nice things.

Pass out Homework.

Teacher 1:
Here is your Homework. Be sure to do it and bring it back next time. Let's see what it says.

(Read aloud.)

If you need help, ask your parents or some other adult in your home.

Skill 16: Handling Name-Calling and Teasing
Role Plays

Situations Target Behaviors	School Problems (Teacher/Peers)	Neighborhood Problems	Sibling Problems	Parent Problems
Listen Carefully	Your teacher is answering your question about the homework. The kid behind you starts whispering that you're stupid, etc.	You're talking to the old lady who lives down the street. Some kids ride by and tease you for talking to the "weird" lady.	Your mom is giving directions to you over the phone while your sister's saying you can't do anything right anyway.	Your sister is helping you with your homework. Your dad says that if you'd study and pay attention in school, you wouldn't be so stupid and helpless.
Treat Others Nicely	You're playing basketball, and you miss a shot. One of your teammates starts yelling at you and says you're a lousy player.	You are at the bus stop waiting for your school bus to come. Two other children are calling you names.	Your little sister is mad at you. She is drawing real ugly pictures, showing them to you, and saying that they're you.	Your dad just told you if you get in any trouble, you're grounded. One of your friends starts making fun of your shirt.
Join in with Others	You're doing an art project. Another child says, "What an ugly picture. You should throw it away; you're wasting paper." You see other kids playing nicely.	You're walking down the street talking to Sue. Some kids call out, "*John* has a girlfriend; *John* loves Sue (etc.)."	You just got home from the barber. Your brother says, "It looks like you got scalped!" Your sister is playing a game you like.	At a big family picnic your aunt asks how you are. Your mom starts nagging about you (dumb, lazy, don't listen, etc.).
Keep a Good Attitude	You're walking down the hall at school. You pass by two kids; they begin laughing and making fun of your clothes.	Some kids are playing ball. You ask if you can play. One says, "You can't hit or catch the ball; I don't want a klutz on my team."	You're playing a game with your brother and a friend. Your brother is losing and says, "You're a cheater and a crummy player, (etc.)."	Your best friend came over to go to the movie. You both put on some makeup, and when you come out, your mom laughs.
Take Responsibility for Self	Two kids cut school during lunch and ask you to join them. When you say "no" they make fun of you for being a chicken.	You're swimming with some friends. They try to talk you into diving off the board, but you don't want to. "Chicken, scaredy-cat!"	You asked to go to the movies, but dad said, "No." Your sister says, "Poor baby, now you'll cry because you didn't get your way."	You lose your allowance. You tell your mom and say you're sorry. She starts yelling at you (you're dumb, irresponsible, etc.).
Stay Calm and Relaxed	You got a neat toy while on vacation. You bring it to school to show your friends, but they all tease you about it.	Your bike has a flat; you ask to borrow a friend's bike. He says, "I wouldn't let you use my bike. You are too clumsy and careless."	You're watching T.V. Your sister comes in and says, "Are you watching that kid show again? That dumb show is for babies (etc.)."	Your dad comes to school to meet your teacher, and when you introduce him, he talks about how clumsy and slow you are.
Solve Problems	On your way home from school some kids start calling you names. "Hey fatso, tubbo, four-eyes, tinsel-teeth (etc.)."	You get a new hat and wear it out to play. Some kids yank your hat off, begin to toss it around, and say how silly it looks.	You crash on your bike. When you ask your brother to help you fix it, he says, "No way; you fix it yourself, you clod."	You're doing your chores, and your mom's in a bad mood. She says "You're so lazy; you never do anything (etc.)."

Skill 16: Handling Name-Calling and Teasing
Activity

The materials needed are:

1. A set of cards, each naming a well-known villain from a movie, cartoon strip, or T.V. series.
2. Small prizes or edible treats.

Have each child pick one card. Tell the children that each person will pretend to be the villain named on the card that he/she has picked. Each villain will take a turn sitting in the middle of the circle. That child will announce his/her "name," and the other children will name-call and tease the villain. Every villain who ignores the name-calling correctly (and *seriously*) earns a prize.

Give Positive Feedback, in addition to prizes, to children who successfully handle the name-calling.

Party Planning During Session 16
Additional Activity

Use this activity during snack time.

The materials needed are:

1. Chalkboard and chalk, or
2. Chart paper and marker.

While the children are eating snack, tell them that you are going to plan a party for your last social skills session. Ask what they think they need for a good party. Write all suggestions of food, drink, and games in categories, on the board or chart for everyone to see. (Behaviors that can be practiced and reinforced at this time include: interrupting the right way, volunteering, and having a good attitude.)

After all suggestions have been made and categories are complete, tell the children that fewer than the total number of suggestions in each category can be brought to the party. (You decide on the specific number.) The children then have to agree on which items to eliminate. (Behaviors that can be practiced and reinforced at this time include: interrupting the right way, compromising, problem solving, and having a good attitude.)

After the children have finalized the party list, tell them what you are willing to bring (if anything), and let them volunteer and sign up for the remaining items. Items that do not receive a signature can be eliminated.

It is helpful to pose the following problem for the children to solve: "What if you tell your parents what you signed up to bring, and they tell you that you can't bring it?"

You may also want to talk about responsibility (child's vs. parents') for making, buying, bringing, etc., party items.

Note: In the demonstration groups the party occurred on the last social skills session and was a substitute for the regularly scheduled snack and activity. You will need to decide on the best arrangement for your setting (see Progress Chart in Chapter 5).

Skill 16: Handling Name-Calling and Teasing
Home Note

Name _____ Instructors _____

During today's lesson we practiced handling name-calling and teasing. When someone called us names or teased us, we practiced keeping calm, ignoring, and walking away if possible. We also used positive self-talk, which is thinking good things about oneself (e.g., "I'm calm. I can handle this. I can ignore").

Today's Objectives	**Target Behaviors**

Today's Objectives

To handle name-calling and teasing, did the child:

	YES	NO
1. Keep a pleasant face?	_____	_____
2. Take a deep breath to get calm?	_____	_____
3. Look away, or walk away if he/she could?	_____	_____
4. Use positive self-talk?	_____	_____

Target Behaviors

Score

A. _____ _____
B. _____ _____
C. _____ _____
D. _____ _____
E. _____ _____

Score, using this scale:
1 = Completely satisfied
2 = Satisfied
3 = Slightly satisfied
4 = Neither satisfied nor dissatisfied
5 = Slightly dissatisfied
6 = Dissatisfied
7 = Completely dissatisfied

The best thing your child did today in social skills was _____
_____

- -

Parents – Please Complete This Section and Return
Skill 16: Handling Name-Calling and Teasing

Name _____

The following objectives and target behaviors refer to those named above. Please mark or score your child in these areas and have him/her return this bottom section with your signature to the next social skills group.

Did your child meet the objectives of today's lesson at least once this week?

	YES	NO
Objective 1	_____	_____
Objective 2	_____	_____
Objective 3	_____	_____
Objective 4	_____	_____

Score your child on his/her target behaviors, using the 1-7 scale above:

Target Behavior A _____
Target Behavior B _____
Target Behavior C _____
Target Behavior D _____
Target Behavior E _____

Parent Signature _____ Date _____

Skill 16: Handling Name-Calling and Teasing
Homework

Name _____

1. What are three things you would do if someone teased you or called you a name?

   a. _____
   _____

   b. _____
   _____

   c. _____
   _____

2. List three examples of positive self-talk that you would say to yourself.

   a. _____
   _____

   b. _____
   _____

   c. _____
   _____

3. What if you did everything right to handle name-calling and teasing, but the other person still called you names. What are two things you could do?

   a. _____
   _____

   b. _____
   _____

4. Did anyone tease you or call you a name this week?
   (Circle one.)   YES   NO

   a. If yes, what did you do? _____
   _____

   b. What did the other person do? _____
   _____

   c. If no, what would you have done if someone had? _____
   _____

Session 17

Skill 17: Saying "No" to Stay Out of Trouble

YOU MAY SUBSTITUTE naturally occurring events (lunch time, art projects, etc.) for items marked with an asterisk. Be sure to incidentally teach the day's skill, target behaviors, and the behaviors listed whether you use these activities or others. Remember that the dialogue provided in the session outlines (except for the lesson itself) is intended to be a model, not read or memorized verbatim. Read the dialogue over for main points and use your own spontaneous style. **Most of the dialogue and instructions are identical from skill to skill. For efficiency you may wish to attend only to the Relaxation Script number and the new information in the Skill Lesson.**

*Homework Completion and Free Play

In addition to today's skill and children's individual target behaviors, give special attention to taking responsibility, solving problems, and following directions (during Homework completion), and joining in, cooperating, problem solving, keeping a good attitude, and following directions (during free play).

Collect Homework and the bottom half of Home Notes; oversee free play and Homework completion or practice time.

Teacher 1:
(Scan papers to see which children have satisfactorily completed Homework; put aside Home Notes to check later.)

(children who completed it), you may go now and choose a game to play. (children who have not completed it), it's time for you to finish the Homework (or practice the skill) so that you can join the others.

(For children who habitually do not bring completed Homework, add more written questions or role play practice so that they finish about the same time as free play ends.)

Review Homework with children.

Teacher 1:
(Have children form a circle on the floor.)

Now let's look at the Homework you have done. I'm glad that (children who brought completed work) did their work at home. (a child who brought it), will you read your answer to Question _____?

(Have several children who brought their work read answers; ask for feedback from others. If you are using the Homework Progress Chart, allow children to color in the whole square or place a sticker in the square or color in part of it, depending on whether they brought completed Homework or finished it during free play.)

*Relaxation Training

In addition to today's skill and children's individual target behaviors, give special attention to keeping a calm body, solving problems, following directions, and keeping hands to self.

Lead relaxation training.

Teacher 1:
We are going to practice relaxing again. Relaxing will help you learn the new skill and help you face any problem.

(Have children find a place on the floor to lie down. Choose one child to turn off the lights.)

(Use Relaxation Script 8.)

Skill Lesson 17

● **Introduce skill and list components.**

Teacher 1:
Today we are going to talk about saying "no" to stay out of trouble. When others try to talk you into doing something you know you shouldn't do, you should say "no." To say "no," you:
- Use a pleasant face and voice.
- Take a deep breath to get calm.
- Look at the person.
- Keep saying "no."
- Suggest something else to do.

If suggesting something else doesn't work, you:
- Ignore and walk away.

. . . .

● **Role play appropriate example.**

Teacher 1:
This is the right way to say "no." I'm at the store after school with my friend. We have no money.
I would really like some of these baseball cards.

Teacher 2:
Just pick some up. If you put them in your pocket, the clerk won't notice.

Teacher 1:
No way. I don't steal. Let's go to my house and see if my mom has any odd jobs she'll pay us to do. We can come back later when we have money.

Teacher 2:
No . . . that's too much trouble. Just put them in your pocket.

Teacher 1:
No. I don't steal.

Teacher 2:
Come on, chicken!

Teacher 1:
(ignores and walks away)

● **Ask children for behavior components of skill.**

Teacher 1:
How did you know that was the right way to say "no"?
(children respond or are prompted)

● **Role play inappropriate example.**

Teacher 1:
This is the wrong way to say "no." I'm at the store after school with a friend. We have no money.
I would really like some of these baseball cards.

Teacher 2:
Just pick some up. If you put them in your pocket, the clerk won't notice.

Teacher 1:
No way. I don't steal. Let's go to my house and see if my mom has any odd jobs she'll pay us to do. We can come back later when we have money.

Teacher 2:
No . . . that's too much trouble. Just put them in your pocket.

Teacher 1:
Well . . . OK.

● **Ask children for behavior components of skill.**

Teacher 1:
What should have happened to make that the right way to say "no"?
(children respond or are prompted)

. . . .

● **Ask children to role play.**

Teacher 1:
Now it is your turn to role play. (Assign role play situation.) I am going to call on someone who has been working really hard in the group by (specific on-task behaviors).
_____ has been working really hard the whole time by (appropriate behaviors) and looks ready to be the first one to role play. _____, this is your role play.

(Describe the role play you have previously selected for this child from the role play sheet behind this session outline. Have each child role play the skill *correctly* at least one time.)

● **Ask children to give Positive Feedback.**

Teacher 1 or 2:
Good role playing. Who can give _____ *some Positive Feedback on his/her role play?*

(Call on child who is volunteering and paying attention.)

. . . .

● **Ask children for rationales for using skill.**

Teacher 1:
Why do you think it is important to say "no" when others are trying to talk you into doing something you know you shouldn't do?
(children respond or are prompted)

Children:
- It keeps you out of trouble.
- You feel better when you make your own decisions and choices.
- Others will trust you more.
- You take responsibility for yourself.

. . . .

● **Lead children through reality check.**

Teacher 1:
Sometimes you might try really hard to say "no," *and this might happen.* I'm at the store after school with a friend. We have no money.
I would really like some of these baseball cards.

Teacher 2:
Just pick some up. If you put them in your pocket, the clerk won't notice.

Teacher 1:
No way. I don't steal. Let's go to my house and see if my mom has any odd jobs she'll pay us to do. We can come back later when we have money.

Teacher 2:
No . . . that's too much trouble. Just put them in your pocket.

Teacher 1:
No, I don't steal.

Teacher 2:
Come on, chicken!

Teacher 1:
(ignores and begins to walk away)

Teacher 2:
You're such a jerk. I'm never going to be your friend again!

Teacher 1:
You just did everything right to say "no." *What should you do if this happens to you?*
(children respond or are prompted)

Children:
- Take a deep breath to get calm.
- Keep a good attitude.
- Walk away.
- Ignore name-calling.
- Find someone else to play with.

---

*Snack Time

In addition to today's skill and children's individual target behaviors, give special attention to following group rules, using conversation skills, cooperating, and solving problems. (Instead of regular snack, you may use party as planned in Session 16.)

Decide which children have earned all of snack.

Children may earn the entire snack or only a smaller portion if they join the snack in progress. Keep in mind how much difficulty a child has had following rules or practicing during the lesson and relaxation time to get an idea of how much time the child might need to practice to compensate for missed opportunities.

Dismiss children who have already earned snack time to the snack table.

Teacher 1:
OK, it's snack time now. (Teacher 2), who do you think has really been earning snack today?

Teacher 2:
Well, _____ has been really following the rules, having a still body, volunteering, and working on (his/her target behavior).

Teacher 1:
Yes, he/she really has. And I think _____ has also done a really good job of (specific behaviors). I'd like (child already named) to go to the snack table and pass out the napkins and (other child named) to go and pass out the cups.

(Continue dismissing children to the snack table by giving Positive Feedback for their accomplishments and assigning them a task at the snack table. If some children have not earned all of snack, have them practice as follows.)

Teacher 1:
_____, you need to sit here with me and practice (volunteering, keeping hands to self, etc.).

151

(Ask children questions from the lesson, have them role play, or do relaxation to give them opportunities to practice behaviors that were problematic during relaxation and/or the lesson. As the children practice, watch for a good attitude and effort in practicing and determine when each child seems to have made up for lost opportunities and achieved an acceptable level of competence in the skill or rule following.)

Ask children to clean up snack area.

Teacher 1:
OK, snack time is over now. We need to clean up. _____, would you get the garbage can and bring it around so everyone can throw away the garbage.

(Use Positive Feedback and other Teaching Strategies for cooperating and following directions during the cleanup.)

---

*Activity Time

In addition to today's skill and children's individual target behaviors, give special attention to following group rules, using conversation skills, cooperating, and solving problems. (Instead of regular activity, you may use party as planned in Session 16.)

Explain activity for today's lesson.

Teacher 1:
It's time for an activity now. Today we're going to (describe activity briefly). This is a time for us to practice our target behaviors and Saying "No" to Stay Out of Trouble.

(Use Activity.)

Ask all the children to help clean up.

Teacher 1:
Now it's time for everyone to help clean up.

(Use Positive Feedback and other Teaching Strategies to help children work well together on cleanup. After cleanup, prompt children to return to circle.)

---

*Home Notes

In addition to today's skill and children's individual target behaviors, give special attention to following group rules and saying nice things.

Divide children into two groups and work on scoring Home Notes.

Teacher 1:
(a child), we are going to talk about how you did during today's session. Who can give (that child) some Positive Feedback and tell him/her good things about how he/she did on (target behavior)?

(Score the top half of the Home Note while the children are giving Positive Feedback. Ask for specific feedback for each of the child's target behaviors and add to it with comments you want to make, pointing out progress and areas needing improvement.)

(same child), now what do you think was the best thing you did in group today?
(child responds or is prompted)

Teacher 1:
That's good.

(Add specific descriptions of strong points.)

You might also try to (suggestions for improvement). Here is your Home Note.

(Repeat sequence with each child.)

---

*New Homework

In addition to today's skill and children's individual target behaviors, give special attention to following group rules and saying nice things.

Pass out Homework.

Teacher 1:

Here is your Homework. Be sure to do it and bring it back next time. Let's see what it says.

(Read aloud.)

If you need help, ask your parents or some other adult in your home.

Relaxation Script 8

(This script may be used in conjunction with Skill 17. Please review the section on relaxation training in Chapter 5 of the Guide.)

Today we'll be learning how to relax while sitting in a chair; that way we will be able to relax without others noticing. We can even relax at our desks at school or while sitting at the dinner table at home. (pause) First, I want you to sit with your bottom flat in the chair and your feet touching the floor. (pause) Your back should be resting comfortably against the back of the chair, your face looking forward, and your eyes open. Your arms should be lying loosely in your lap. (pause) As I count to three, breathe in slowly, and as you breathe out, think the words "I AM CALM." (count aloud slowly) One . . . two . . . three. (pause) Relax. Now your body is ready to relax.

Think about your face. If there is any tightness in your forehead, mouth, or eyes, let them go smooth. (pause) As I count to three, breathe in slowly, and as you breathe out, think the words "I AM CALM." (count aloud slowly) One . . . two . . . three. (pause) Relax.

Think about your shoulders. If they are feeling tight, let them go soft and loose. (pause) As I count to three, breathe in slowly, and as you breathe out, think the words "I AM CALM." (count aloud slowly) One . . . two . . . three. (pause) Relax.

Now think about your arms and hands. If they are feeling tight, let them relax loosely in your lap. (pause) As I count to three, breathe in slowly, and as you breathe out, think the words "I AM CALM." (count aloud slowly) One . . . two . . . three. (pause) Relax.

Think about your stomach and back. If they are feeling upset or tight, let them go soft and loose. (pause) As I count to three, breathe in slowly, and as you breathe out, think the words "I AM CALM." (count aloud slowly) One . . . two . . . three. (pause) Relax.

Now think about your legs and feet. If they are feeling tight or wiggly, let them relax. Your legs feel calm and loose. (pause) As I count to three, breathe in slowly, and as you breathe out, think the words "I AM CALM." (count aloud slowly) One . . . two . . . three. (pause) Relax.

Now that your body is relaxed, I want you to imagine yourself having a problem with another child. You and a friend are playing a game and having a good time. Your body feels relaxed and happy. Another child comes over and tries to offer the two of you a cigarette. Your body begins to feel tense and nervous. Think about how your body feels; your arms, stomach, and face may feel tense. (pause) If any parts of your body feel tense, let them relax. (pause) As I count to three, breathe in slowly, and as you breathe out, think the words "I AM CALM." (count aloud slowly) One . . . two . . . three. (pause) Relax. One more time, keep your body loose and relaxed and imagine someone trying to get you to shoplift something for him. (pause) As I count to three, breathe in slowly, and as you breathe out, think the words "I AM CALM." (count aloud slowly) One . . . two . . . three. (pause) Relax. Now you can keep calm and say "no" in a nice way.

Now I want you to imagine yourself at a friend's house. He tells you he'll give you some of his father's whiskey. You are afraid he won't like you if you say "no." Your body begins to feel tense and nervous. Think about how your body feels; your arms, stomach, and face may feel tense. (pause) If any parts of your body feel tense, let them relax. (pause) As I count to three, breathe in slowly, and as you breathe out, think the words "I AM CALM." (count aloud slowly) One . . . two . . . three. (pause) Relax.

One more time, keep your body loose and relaxed and think of keeping your body calm when you are nervous. (pause) As I count to three, breathe in slowly, and as you breathe out, think the words "I AM CALM." (count aloud slowly) One . . . two . . . three. (pause) Relax. Now you can keep calm and say "no" in a nice way.

Now your body feels calm and relaxed. The next time you find yourself having a problem with someone else and your body feels upset, nervous, or angry, remember to take a slow deep breath and relax your body. When your body is calm, it is easier to take care of the problems you have with other people.

Skill 17: Saying "No" to Stay Out of Trouble
Role Plays

Situations / Target Behaviors	School Problems (Teacher/Peers)	Neighborhood Problems	Sibling Problems	Parent Problems
Listen Carefully	The teacher says anyone who does not clean his desk will not go to recess. A bully tells you to clean his desk for him.	The last time you cut across the neighbor's lawn on your bike, she asked you not to. Your friend wants you to do it with him now.	Your sister asked you to watch her bike while she runs in the store. Some kids come by and ask to ride it around the block just once.	Your mom told you to be home by 6:00. Your friend wants you to go to the store with her. It's 5:45 now.
Treat Others Nicely	The kids in your class are hiding books and things from the teacher. They want you to join in.	Your friends are all bugging a kid down the street. They want you to join in.	Your little brother just got glasses. Your friend thinks it would be funny to take them and hide them.	You know your mom is looking forward to making pies with the cherries on her tree. Some kids want to eat them now.
Join in with Others	Your friends are joking about what they want to do at recess – maybe take a ball from the first-graders. You want to play.	Your friend has asked you to join her club. In order to join, you have to steal something from the drugstore.	Your brother broke his leg while skiing. Your best friend thinks it would be fun to steal his crutches.	You are a member of a ball team. Your mom told you to come right home. Your teammate wants you to go to a game tonight.
Keep a Good Attitude	Some kids try to get you to throw rocks at the school window. You say "no" and they threaten not to be your friends anymore.	Some kids want you to smoke a cigarette with them. They call you a chicken when you say "no."	Your sister wants you to go to the 7-11 with her and play electronic games. Mom told you to stay home and finish your chores.	Your mom says to babysit your little brother at home. Your pal suggests you bring him along to a ball game. You can't.
Take Responsibility for Self	Your friend wants you to cut school and meet him at the river to fish.	While playing softball, you break the neighbor's window. Your friends suggest that you say someone else did it.	Your brother suggests that you try some of your dad's whiskey.	Your dad says you have to do yard work every day this week. He's out of town. Your pal suggests you take the day off.
Stay Calm and Relaxed	Your friends want you to spray paint the school. You say "no," and they call you a sissy.	A kid who always bullies you at school asks you if he can come to your birthday party. Your mom says, "Definitely not!"	You're picnicking at the lake, and your sister suggests that you swim across. She says you're a big chicken if you don't.	Your dad leaves you to babysit your sister while he goes to the store. Your friends ask you to go swimming with them.
Solve Problems	The teacher told you the wrong page to study, and you failed the test. A kid says she'll help you change your grade.	Some kids want you to go to a movie with them. You know your mom wouldn't want you to see that movie.	Your mom took your bike away for a week. You're late for school, and your sister suggests that you ride your bike.	You lost the money you had saved to go to a movie. Your friend suggests that you take some from your mom's purse.

Skill 17: Saying "No" to Stay Out of Trouble
Activity

The materials needed are:

1. List of super villains.
2. List of evil plots.
3. Super hero stickers (optional).

Each child takes the part of a super villain. Divide the children in pairs and have them take turns trying to talk each other into helping with an evil plot.

Children who say "no" appropriately may win a super hero sticker to take home.

Watch for instances of saying "no" appropriately and use Positive Feedback in response. Use other Teaching Strategies as needed to help the children refine the skill.

Skill 17: Saying "No" to Stay Out of Trouble
Home Note

Name _____ Instructors _____

During today's lesson we practiced saying "no" to stay out of trouble. We do this when someone tries to talk us into doing something we know we shouldn't do. It's not easy, and sometimes we may have to walk away from the person.

Today's Objectives	Target Behaviors

Today's Objectives

To say "no" to stay out of trouble, did the child:

	YES	NO
1. Use a pleasant face and voice?	____	____
2. Take a deep breath to get calm?	____	____
3. Look at the person?	____	____
4. Keep saying "no"?	____	____
5. Suggest something else to do?	____	____

If suggesting something else didn't work, did the child:

| 6. Ignore and walk away? | ____ | ____ |

Target Behaviors

Score

A. _____ ____
B. _____ ____
C. _____ ____
D. _____ ____
E. _____ ____

Score, using this scale:
1 = Completely satisfied
2 = Satisfied
3 = Slightly satisfied
4 = Neither satisfied nor dissatisfied
5 = Slightly dissatisfied
6 = Dissatisfied
7 = Completely dissatisfied

The best thing your child did today in social skills was _____
_____

- -

Parents – Please Complete This Section and Return
Skill 17: Saying "No" to Stay Out of Trouble

Name _____

The following objectives and target behaviors refer to those named above. Please mark or score your child in these areas and have him/her return this bottom section with your signature to the next social skills group.

Did your child meet the objectives of today's lesson at least once this week?

	YES	NO
Objective 1	____	____
Objective 2	____	____
Objective 3	____	____
Objective 4	____	____
Objective 5	____	____
Objective 6	____	____

Score your child on his/her target behaviors, using the 1-7 scale above:

Target Behavior A _____
Target Behavior B _____
Target Behavior C _____
Target Behavior D _____
Target Behavior E _____

Parent Signature _____ Date _____

Skill 17: Saying "No" to Stay Out of Trouble
Homework

Name _____

1. When someone asks you to do something you know is wrong, what are three things you can do?

   a. _____

   _____

   b. _____

   _____

   c. _____

   _____

2. Why is it important to stay calm? _____

   _____

3. If the person keeps trying to talk you into doing something wrong, what should you do? _____

   _____

4. This week did someone ask you to do something you were not allowed to do?
   (Circle one.)   YES   NO

   a. If yes, what did the person ask you to do? _____

   _____

   b. What did you do and say? _____

   _____

   c. What happened? _____

   _____

   d. If no, what would you have done and said if someone had? _____

   _____